Roadside Illustrated

Signpost Up Ahead, The East

A Pictorial Tour of Billboards, Neon, Road Signs and More

Stephen H. Provost

SIGNPOST UP AHEAD, THE EAST

All material © 2023 Stephen H. Provost
Cover concept and design: Stephen H. Provost
Cover photograph: Stephen H. Provost
Back cover: Stephen H. Provost
All contemporary photographs © 2013-2023 Stephen H. Provost
Historical images are in the public domain, except where noted

No part of this book may be reproduced, or stored in a retrieval system, or transmitted in any form or by any means, electronic, mechanical, photocopying, recording, or otherwise, without the express written permission of the publisher.

Dragon Crown Books 2023

All rights reserved.

ISBN: 978-1-949971-36-1

Dedication

To anyone who's ever played the alphabet game on a road trip, stopped at a roadside attraction, or been lured off the road by a super-cool neon sign.

Acknowledgments

Thanks to Sharon Stora for her support, proofreading and marketing assistance.

Contents

Introduction   7

Barn to Be Wild	11
Signs on the Side	33
Post Those Bills	77
This Way, That Far	139
You've Arrived	183
Lighting Up the Night	205
New Heights	243

Front cover photo by Stephen H. Provost
Parkette Drive In, Lexington, Kentucky

Back cover photo by Stephen H. Provost:
Donna Fargo Highway, North Carolina Route 103, somewhere between Mt. Airy and the Virginia state line

Introduction photo by Stephen H. Provost:
Wendover Avenue, Greensboro, North Carolina

Author photo by Stephen H. Provost:
In front of faced wall signs for Pepsi and Wrigley's gum, downtown Durham, North Carolina

SIGNPOST UP AHEAD, THE EAST

More Reading

America's Historic Highways

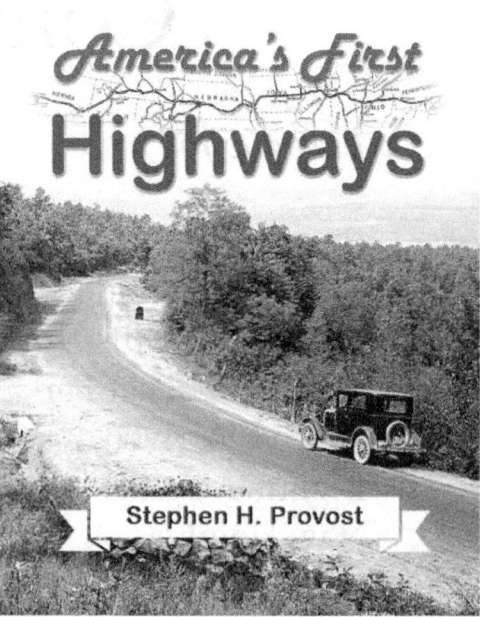

California's Historic Highways

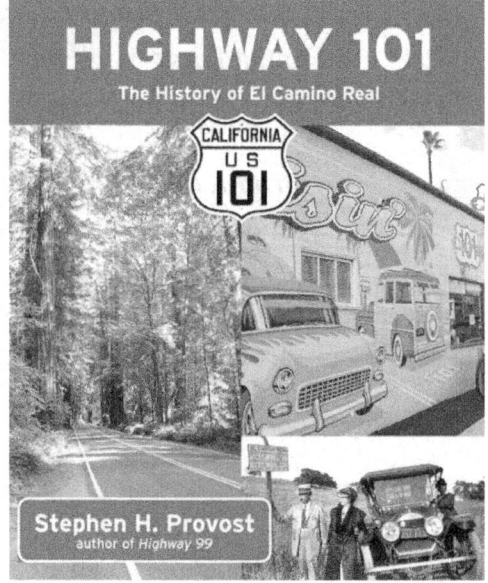

Signposts Up Ahead, The East

STEPHEN H. PROVOST

SIGNPOST UP AHEAD, THE EAST

Introduction

You can't drive far on a U.S. highway or byway before coming across something to read. It might be a traffic sign, a billboard, a neon sign, or even a personalized license plate.

If you've ever played the "alphabet game" — trying to find letters in alphabetical order on signs and license plates during a road trip — you know it doesn't take long to get from A to Z.

When I set out to create a picture book of signs, I quickly realized how many there were: far too many for a single book. Indeed, it would be impossible to cover the vast variety of signs seen by the roadside in an encyclopedia; a library might do it. So I had to settle for a representative sample — even as I expanded this project into two volumes as part of my *Roadside Illustrated* series.

As I've lived and traveled in both the eastern (Virginia) and western (California, Nevada) United States, it seemed natural to break this project up geographically. Choosing the Mississippi River as my dividing line, I produced the first volume, "Signpost Up Ahead, The West" before turning my attention back to the East Coast, where I lived for three years before returning west in 2022.

There are differences between East and West. Las Vegas has neon galore, on and off the strip; the Big Apple has Times Square. The East has turnpikes, something you don't see as much out west (where they're called toll roads). You'll find Pure gas station signs in Virginia, but not Nevada. Billboard companies are different, too.

Boards where bills were posted got their start in the East. And there are a few barn-side ads in the west, but far more remain in the northeast, many of them along the old Lincoln Highway corridor and sprinkled across rural Pennsylvania and Ohio — so many, in fact, that they warranted their own chapter here.

Having taken a wealth of photos for previous books on highway history, I had a number of unused shots from which to choose. I've supplemented these with new photos taken specifically for this book, and with public domain photos from sources such as the Florida and North Carolina state archives; the National Archives; the Library of Congress; the University of Pittsburgh; and other sources. The result is a collection of hundreds of photos in several categories.

Part of the fun was finding out information about signs that aren't there anymore, some unfortunately so. Things can change along our nation's roads, with iconic sites and familiar signs vanishing in the name of progress or at the behest of new landowners. The Parkette Drive In sign in Lexington depicted on the front is one example: It was a preeminent example of '50s drive-in neon, a fixture along the Circle Road for some 70 years, but it was torn down a couple of years after that picture was taken. I feel fortunate to have been able to photograph it.

This book is intended to capture as much of our roadside history as possible by including a representative sample of signage across seven categories. As with the other works in this series, the dates on the photos refer to the year in which they were taken.

SIGNPOST UP AHEAD, THE EAST

I invite you to enjoy this pictorial trip along highways, city streets, and rural roads as they once appeared, and as they appear today, including famed scenic roads such as the Blue Ridge Parkway, Lincoln Highway, and Cumberland Road. The roads of the East are different from those in the far-flung West, but they're no less fascinating and just as beautiful.

I

Barn to Be Wild (of the building)

Pennsylvania 1939

The Summit Hotel in Uniontown sought to attract travelers with the bed of silent film actor John Gilbert, known as "The Great Lover"; the French phrase translates as "shamed be whoever thinks bad of it"

Library of Congress

SIGNPOST UP AHEAD, THE EAST

Kentucky 2021

Rock City, a tourist attraction on Lookout Mountain in Georgia, advertised far and wide, including on this barn south of Bardstown on U.S. Highway 31E

Stephen H. Provost

STEPHEN H. PROVOST

Another Rock City ad on a barn in Kentucky, this one on U.S. Highway 31W

Stephen H. Provost

Ohio 1938

A barn near Columbus boosts Maplewood Farm in Kirkersville, about 25 miles to the east on U.S. 40, as well as jack-of-all-trades H. Lee Emerson, a funeral director who sold furniture and had an ambulance service

Ben Shahn, Library of Congress

Indiana 2018

Mail Pouch Tobacco painted signs on the side of barns like this one on State Route 62 east of Lanesville from 1891 to 1992

Stephen H. Provost

By the 1960s, Mail Pouch Tobacco had about 20,000 barn signs in 22 states, including this one east of Lanesville on State Route 62

Stephen H. Provost

Ohio 2018

Some Mail Pouch ads aren't as well-maintained, as this one near Minerva, Ohio, demonstrates

Stephen H. Provost

Ohio 2018

This old Mail Pouch sign on U.S. Highway 52 in Manchester has also seen better days; barn owners initially received a dollar or two to display the signs, with the company doing the painting

Stephen H. Provost

Ohio 2018

Several Mail Pouch barns, such as this one, can be found in the Canton area, with many owners keeping them preserved with new paint as needed

Stephen H. Provost

Indiana 2018

A large Mail Pouch barn on State Route 62, part of the Ohio River Scenic Byway, invites potential Mail Pouch customers to "treat yourself to the best"

Stephen H. Provost

Ohio 2018

Some barns, such as this one on the Lincoln Highway near Canton, carried an ad for Kentucky Club Pipe Tobacco in addition to a Mail Pouch ad

Stephen H. Provost

Ads for various tonics and remedies for colds, fever, chills, and even malaria are plastered on a barn in Natchez

Ben Shahn, Library of Congress

Fuller Goodman Co. advertised bird roofs, asphalt shingles, and roll roofings on this barn near New Lisbon

Ben Shahn, Library of Congress

Illinois 2018

A sign off Route 66 near Cayuga, Illinois, alerts travelers to Meramec Caverns, a nearly five-mile system of caves in the Ozarks near Stanton, Missouri

Stephen H. Provost

STEPHEN H. PROVOST

Indiana 2018

Some barns are still used to promote businesses, as these more modern ads on a Route 66 barn near Tell City illustrate

Stephen H. Provost

North Carolina 1936

The Hotel Wilrik in Sanford plastered some big lettering on the side of this barn, including its rates of $1.50 to $2.50 a day, directions, and a boast that "our food has made us popular"

Albert Barden, State Archives of North Carolina

Mail Pouch wasn't the only chewing tobacco to utilize barn ads; here, Red Man and Chew Tub share space on a Lancaster County barn with ads for "World's Exposition Shows"

Dick Sheldon, Library of Congress

Barn ads were a common feature of the scenery on Ohio and Pennsylvania highways and byways; here a company called Lerch advertised dry cleaning and made-to-measure suits on U.S. 40 in central Ohio

Dick Sheldon, Library of Congress

Virginia 1936

Not all barn signs were painted on; some were plastered on, such as these for the Downie Bros. Circus and Morton Salt in the Roanoke area

Walker Evans, Library of Congress

Virginia 1936

Another poster advertising the Downie Bros. Wild Animal Circus, this one in Lynchburg a day earlier; Andrew Downie McPhee, who pioneered the "truck show," started this operation in 1926, and Charles Sparks took over four years later

Walker Evans, Library of Congress

II

Signs on the Side (of the building)

Pennsylvania 1921

Three painted-on billboards (two for political candidates) share a wall at the junction of Diamond, Ferry, and Liberty in Pittsburgh

University of Pittsburgh

Ohio 2018

A building along Tuscawaras Road at Brown Avenue in Canton promotes Mail Pouch Tobacco alongside other faded ads

Stephen H. Provost

STEPHEN H. PROVOST

New York 1901

This building on Buffalo's Main Street touted everything from cigars to artificial limbs

Detroit Publishing Company, Library of Congress

Virginia 2021

Coca-Cola plastered its ads on the sides of many buildings, such as this one at 535 Main Street (State Route 293) in Danville

Stephen H. Provost

Pennsylvania 1913

The Chamberlain Company needed a three-story building to advertise all its products, including insecticides, fumigators, and disinfectants, at Grant and Sixth streets in Pittsburgh

University of Pittsburgh

SIGNPOST UP AHEAD, THE EAST

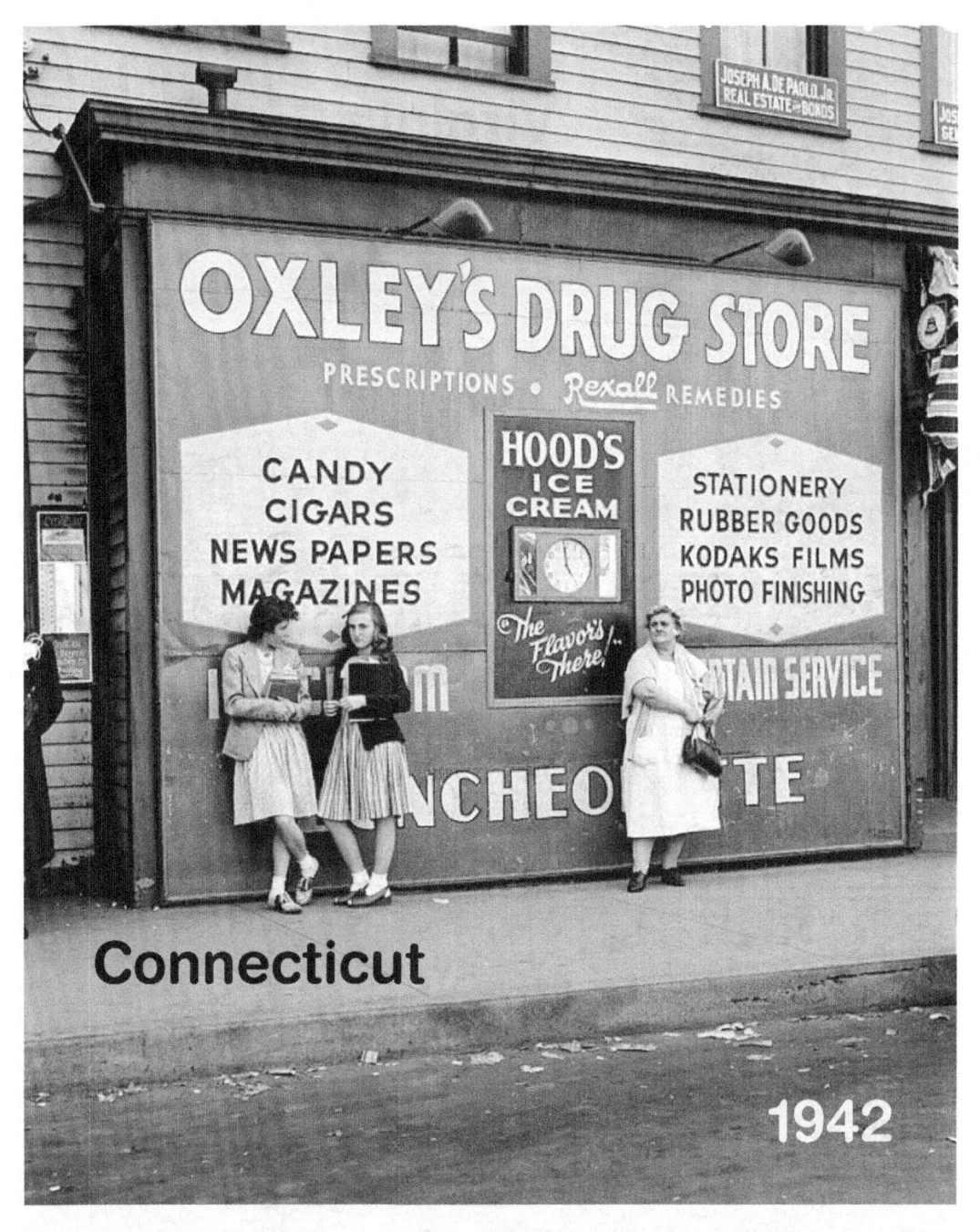

Connecticut

1942

A woman and two schoolgirls wait outside Oxley's Drug Store and Luncheonette in Southington, which used this sign to cover its storefront before it opened

Fenno Jacobs, Library of Congress

Virginia 2020

Shumate and Jessie Furniture is long gone, but the faded sign remains above a more recent circus mural in Martinsville

Stephen H. Provost

SIGNPOST UP AHEAD, THE EAST

Tennessee 2021

F.G. Pitzer sold dry goods, notions, women's hats, cloaks, and carpets at the northeast corner of Piedmont Avenue and State Street in Bristol

Stephen H. Provost

New Jersey 1904

Green's Hotel on the Atlantic City Boardwalk provided guests with a "European plan" along with hot and cold seawater baths

Detroit Publishing Company

North Carolina 2022

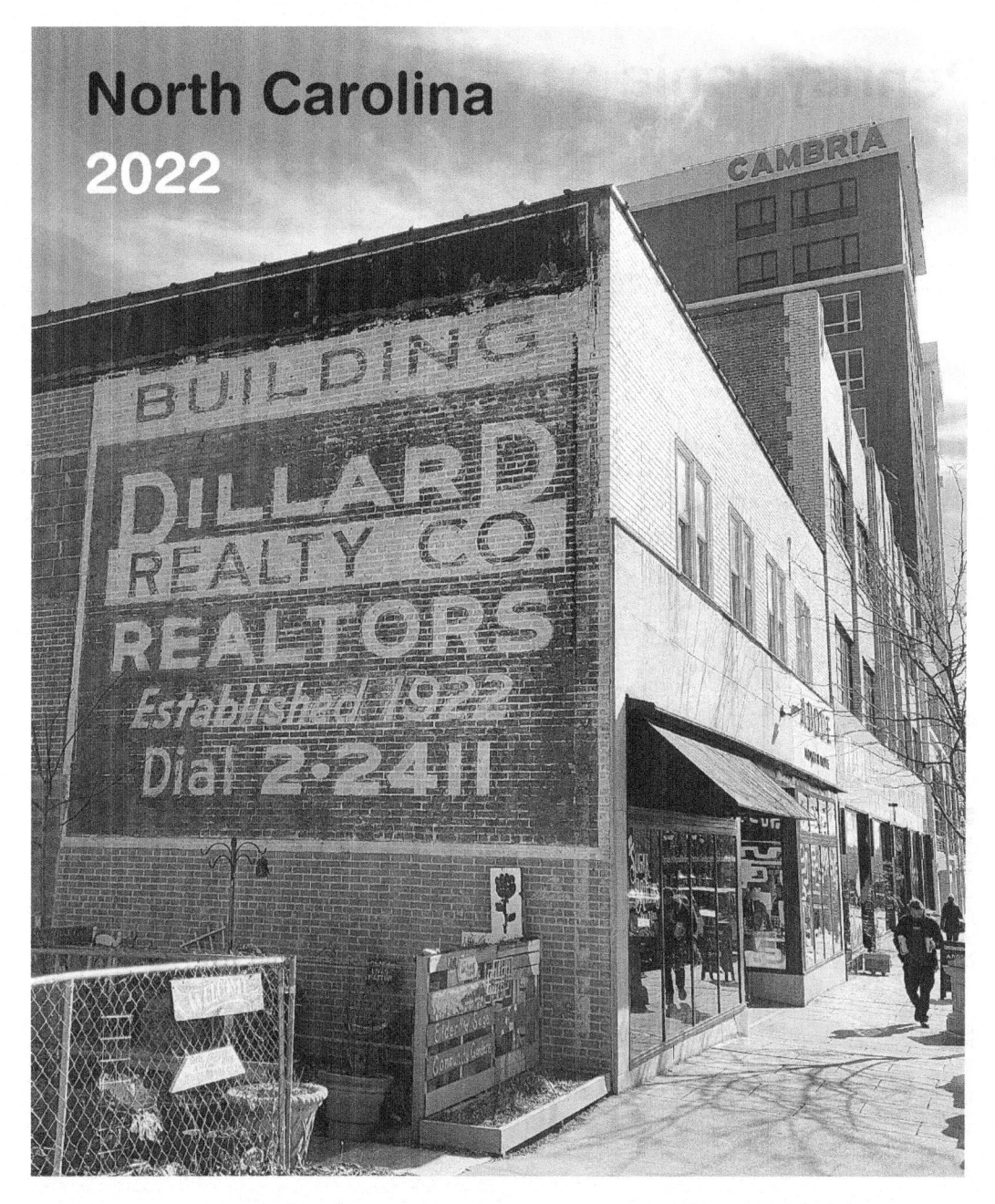

The age of this sign in Asheville for Dillard Realty Co. (established 1922) is betrayed by its five-digit phone number, common during the mid-20th century

Stephen H. Provost

Pennsylvania 1935

Mail Pouch Tobacco didn't limit itself to rural barns; here it appears on a building on Beaver Avenue in Pittsburgh, next to a sign for a confectionary

University of Pittsburgh

SIGNPOST UP AHEAD, THE EAST

Pennsylvania 1935

Another Mail Pouch wall sign on Pittsburgh's Beaver Avenue appeared alongside an ad for Aunt Hannah's Bread and above a billboard for a Jack Benny stage show featuring Mary Livingston

University of Pittsburgh

STEPHEN H. PROVOST

North Carolina 2022

The Camel Pawn Shop, "Home of Low Prices" on Liberty Street **in Winston-Salem was established in 1931**

Stephen H. Provost

A circus parade passes in front of the DeSoto Hotel in Sarasota, which advertised Oleander Ice Cream (a Florida company founded in 1930), during filming of "The Greatest Show on Earth"

State Library and Archives of Florida

STEPHEN H. PROVOST

Pennsylvania 1935

Seven or more billboards share the side of the McGeagh Building on Bigelow Boulevard at Grant Street in Pittsburgh

University of Pittsburgh

Illinois 2018

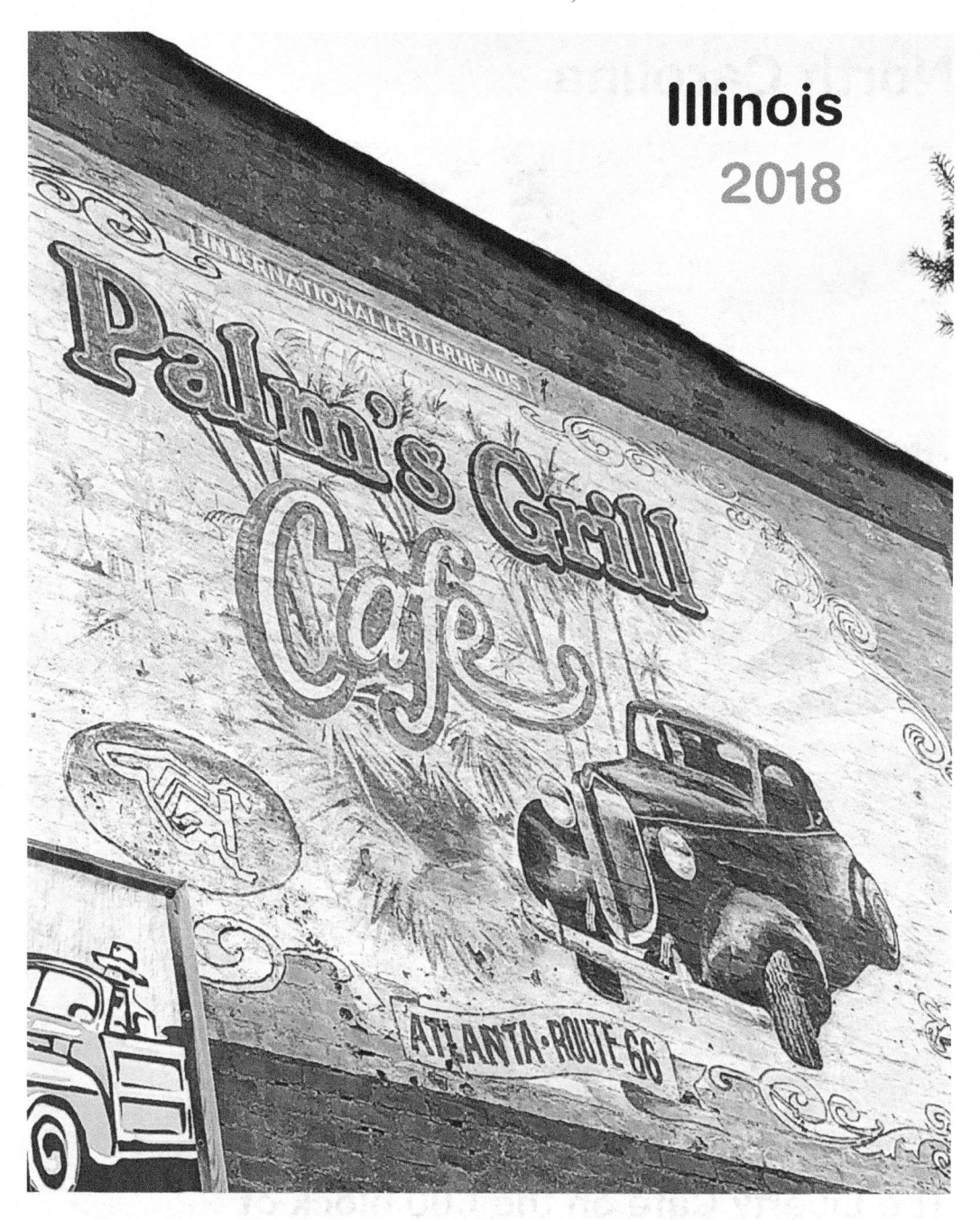

Palm's Grill Café on Route 66 in Atlanta (Illinois, not Georgia) opened in 1934, featuring steak and chicken dinners; nightly dancing; and club parties

Stephen H. Provost

North Carolina 2022

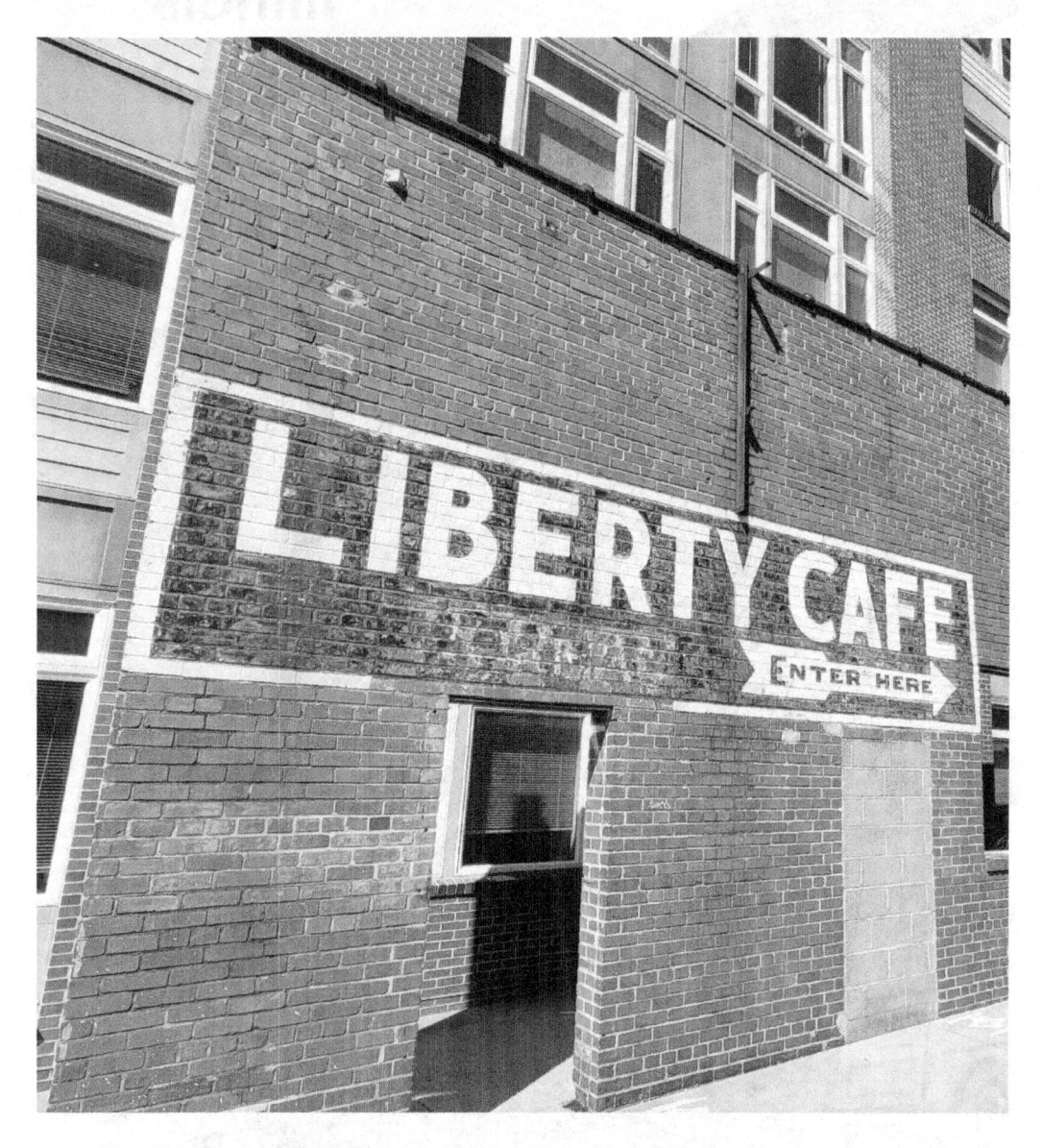

The Liberty Café on the 600 block of Rigsbee Avenue in Durham was part of a tobacco auction warehouse that served customers 24 hours a day at that location starting in the 1940s

Stephen H. Provost

A faded sign in the Five Forks neighborhood of Danville advertises the Bagby Equipment Co., locally owned and founded in 1945

Stephen H. Provost

STEPHEN H. PROVOST

Illinois 2018

Painted ads for baled hay, coal, and pianos share space with a billboard for Busch Beer in Normal on Route 66

Stephen H. Provost

SIGNPOST UP AHEAD, THE EAST

Pennsylvania 1941

Hamburg Brothers was a family-owned appliance and electronics dealer in Pittsburgh, advertised here on a building at Penn Avenue and Barbeau Street

University of Pittsburgh

STEPHEN H. PROVOST

West Virginia 2022

Andrews Floor & Wall Covering covered its own wall in Charleston, West Virginia, with a distinctly modern sign featuring a website

Stephen H. Provost

Virginia 2020

An old Holsum Bread sign on the Central Pharmacy Building in Danville's Five Forks neighborhood only partially survives

Stephen H. Provost

Indiana 2018

Brick walls were popular surfaces for painted signs, as illustrated by this one for Finch & Gage Tailor Made Clothing on Route 66 in Grandview, Indiana; when this photo was taken, the building housed a Masonic Lodge

Stephen H. Provost

SIGNPOST UP AHEAD, THE EAST

Pennsylvania 1933

Old Gold Cigarettes, introduced in 1926 by Lorillard, proclaimed there was "not a cough in a carload" of its smokers on this sign looking east on Bigelow Boulevard in Pittsburgh

University of Pittsburgh

North Carolina 2022

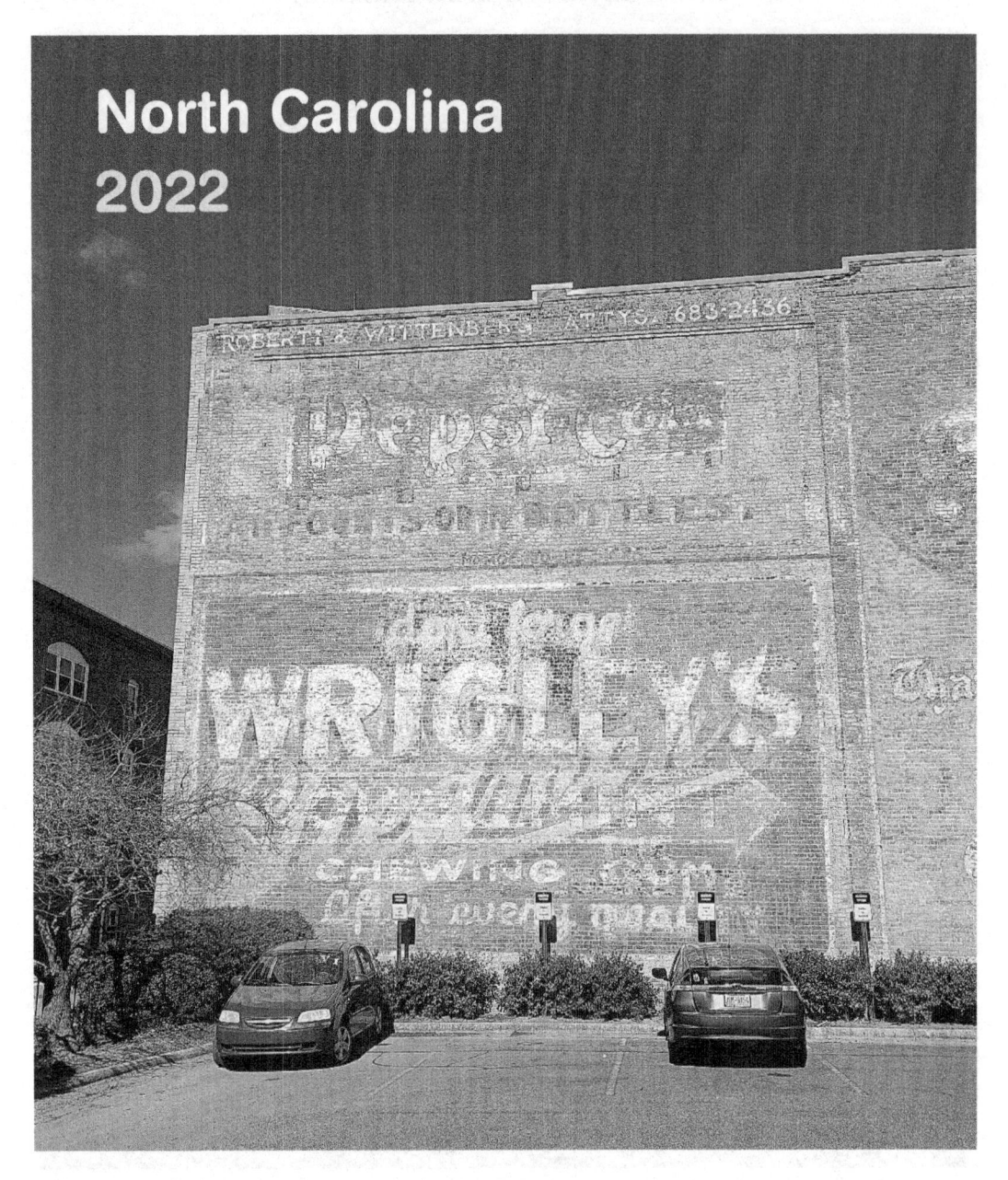

Two or more companies often shared large brick walls, such as this one in Durham, which featured ads for Pepsi Cola and Wrigley's Chewing Gum (recommended "after every meal")

Stephen H. Provost

Another Pepsi sign shares space with a Uneeda Biscuit sign and an ad for the Virginia Carriage Factory in Roanoke

Stephen H. Provost

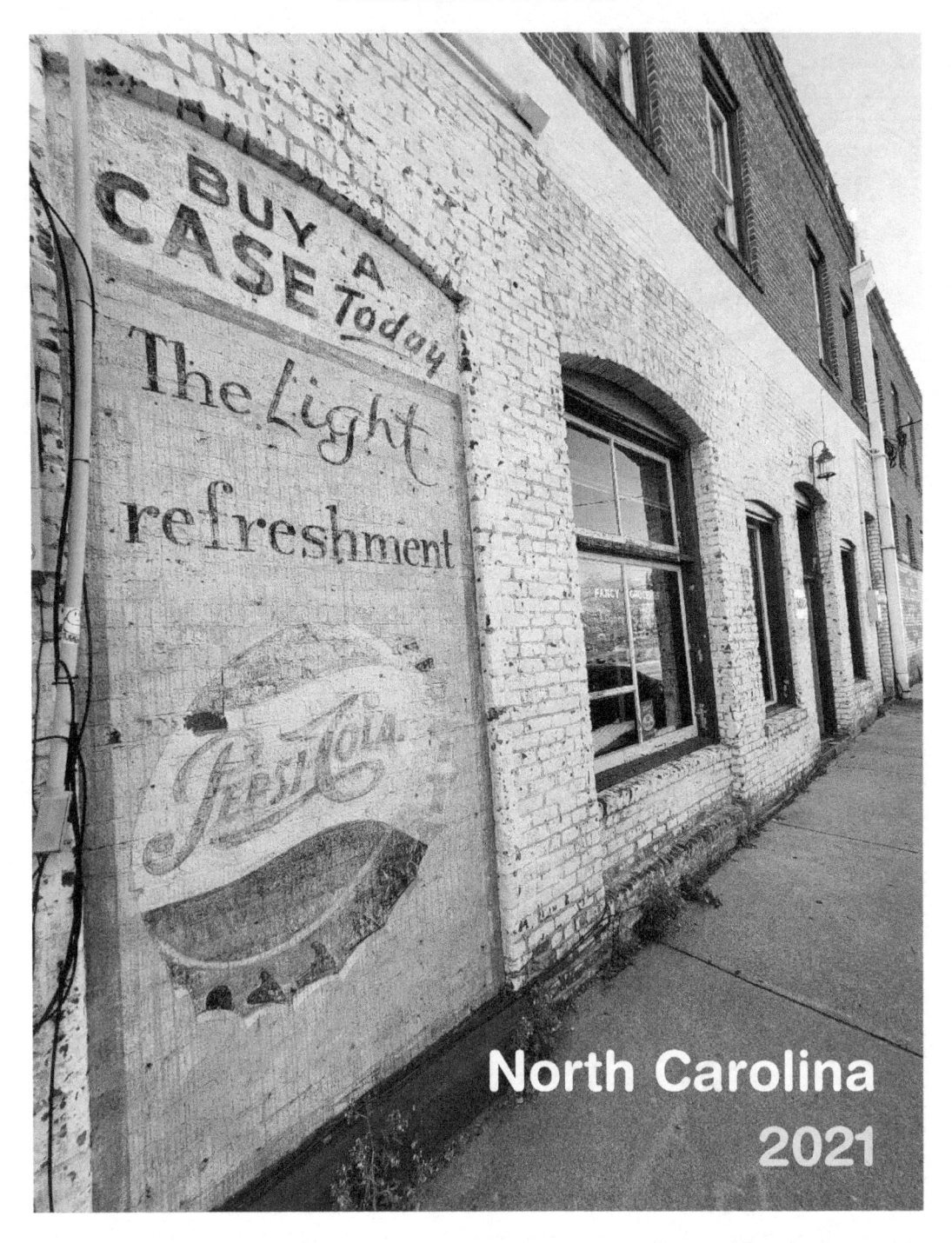

An old painted Pepsi sign adorns a building on Burke Street at Brookstown Avenue in Winston-Salem

Stephen H. Provost

Ohio 1938

Orange Crush was the flavor of the day at Bob's Place roadside lunchroom in Central Ohio, where you could also get pure pork sausage

Bob Shahn, Library of Congress

Bubble Up hawked its 5-cent lemon-lime soda on a building above a Westinghouse billboard on Bigelow Boulevard near Seventh Avenue in Pittsburgh

University of Pittsburgh

SIGNPOST UP AHEAD, THE EAST

Virginia

2021

Royal Crown Cola was featured on the side of this 1910 grocery store on Salem Avenue **in Roanoke**

Stephen H. Provost

North Carolina 2021

You could get Coca-Cola for 5 cents a bottle once upon a time in Mt. Airy, inspiration for Andy Griffith's Mayberry, according to this well-preserved sign

Stephen H. Provost

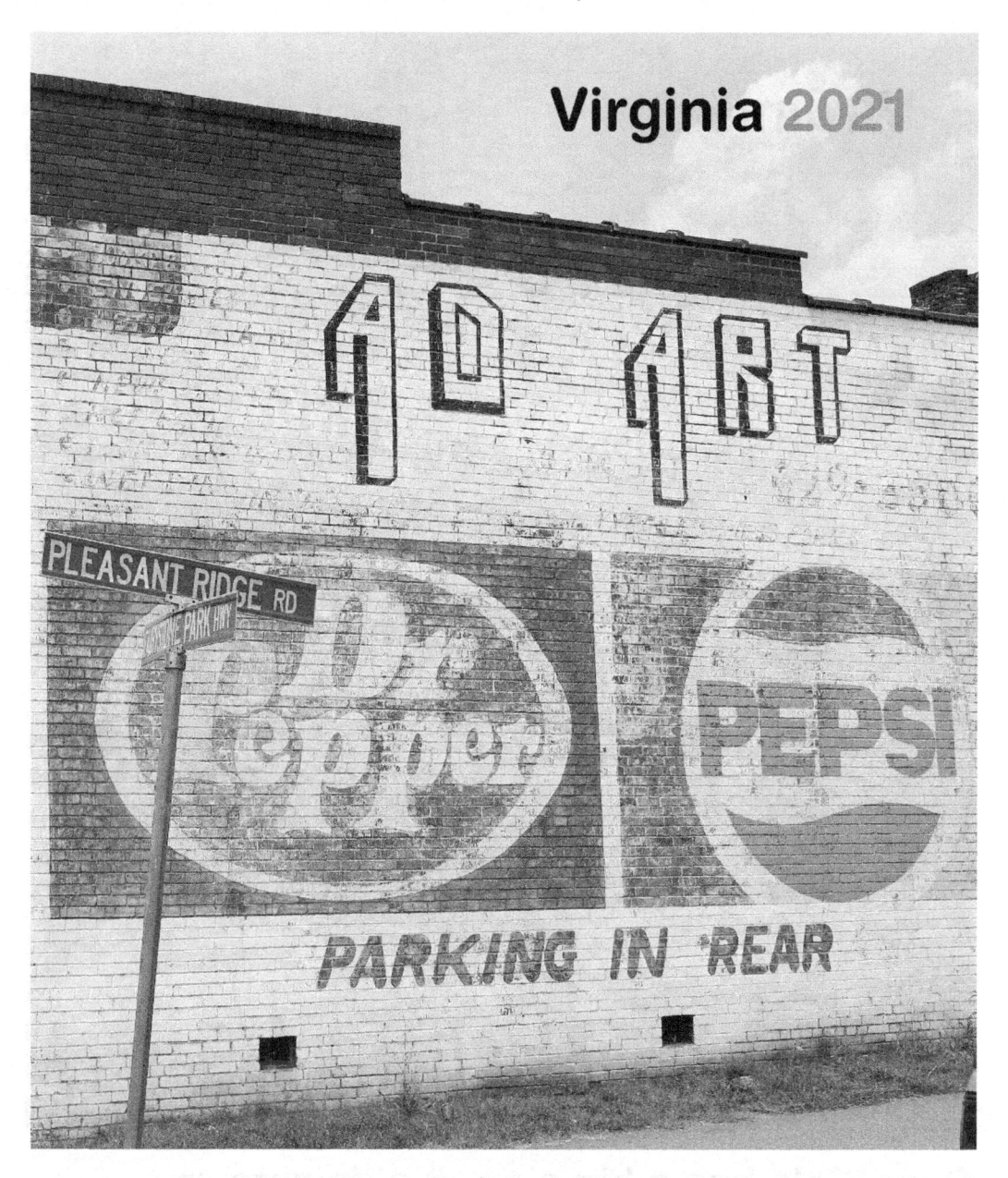

This wall touted Dr Pepper and Pepsi on the Fairystone Park Highway (State Route 57) in Bassett, home to the well-known furniture company

Stephen H. Provost

Virginia 2021

Coca-Cola has a big sign at a downtown parking lot in Roanoke, but the city is far better known for its enthusiastic embrace of Dr Pepper

Stephen H. Provost

SIGNPOST UP AHEAD, THE EAST

Missouri 2018

A home's outer wall serves as a suitable spot for a Coca-Cola sign on Garrison Avenue, aka Route 66, in Carthage

Stephen H. Provost

STEPHEN H. PROVOST

Pennsylvania 1912

A Haugh & Keenan Storage ad on Ross and Sixth streets in Pittsburgh was already fading when this photo was taken showing billboard ads for whiskey, Mother's Oats, and a concert

University of Pittsburgh

SIGNPOST UP AHEAD, THE EAST

Virginia 2021

An older sign in Roanoke advertises Agnew Seed, the oldest such store in Virginia, dating all the way back to 1897

Stephen H. Provost

Maryland 1949

Drive-ins like this one in Elkridge, Maryland, used giant lettering on the back of their big screens to promote themselves

National Archives

Massachusetts 1984

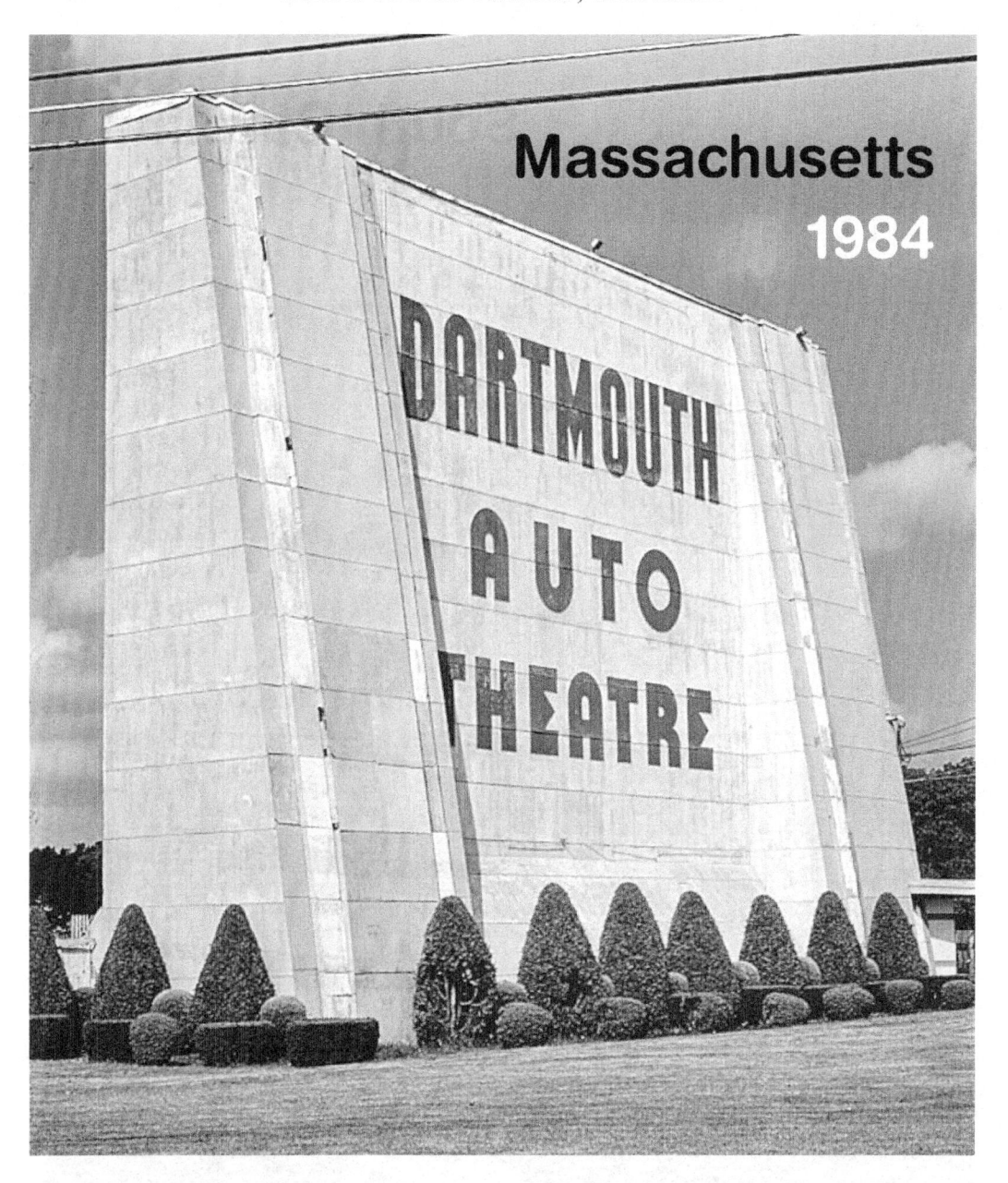

The Dartmouth Auto Theatre off State Route 6 **in Dartmouth had a sturdy screen, to say the least; it opened in 1941 and was renamed the Dartmouth Drive-In by 1955 before eventually being demolished**

John Margolies, Library of Congress

South Carolina
1952

The Clover Leaf Theatre off U.S. Highway 1 in Augusta, South Carolina, was built in 1951 and accommodated 776 cars for its single screen

T.W. Kines, National Archives

South Carolina 1950

The Alta Vista Drive-In opened in 1947 on U.S. Route 1 (Two Notch Road) and was renamed the Twilite seven years later, then finally the Starlite in 1980

T.W. Kines, National Archives

Vermont 1936

Advertisers used whatever surface was handy to get drivers' attention; in this case, it was a large rock on the side of the road near Albany, Vermont

Carl Mydans, Library of Congress

Florida 1931

Streetcars offered another popular surface for ads, such as these in Tampa

State Library and Archives of Florida

III

Post Those Bills: Billboards Galore

Ohio 1936

Circus posters, such as these seen along U.S. Highway 40 in Central Ohio, were among the earliest bills posted on boards

Ben Shahn, Library of Congress

Illinois 1941

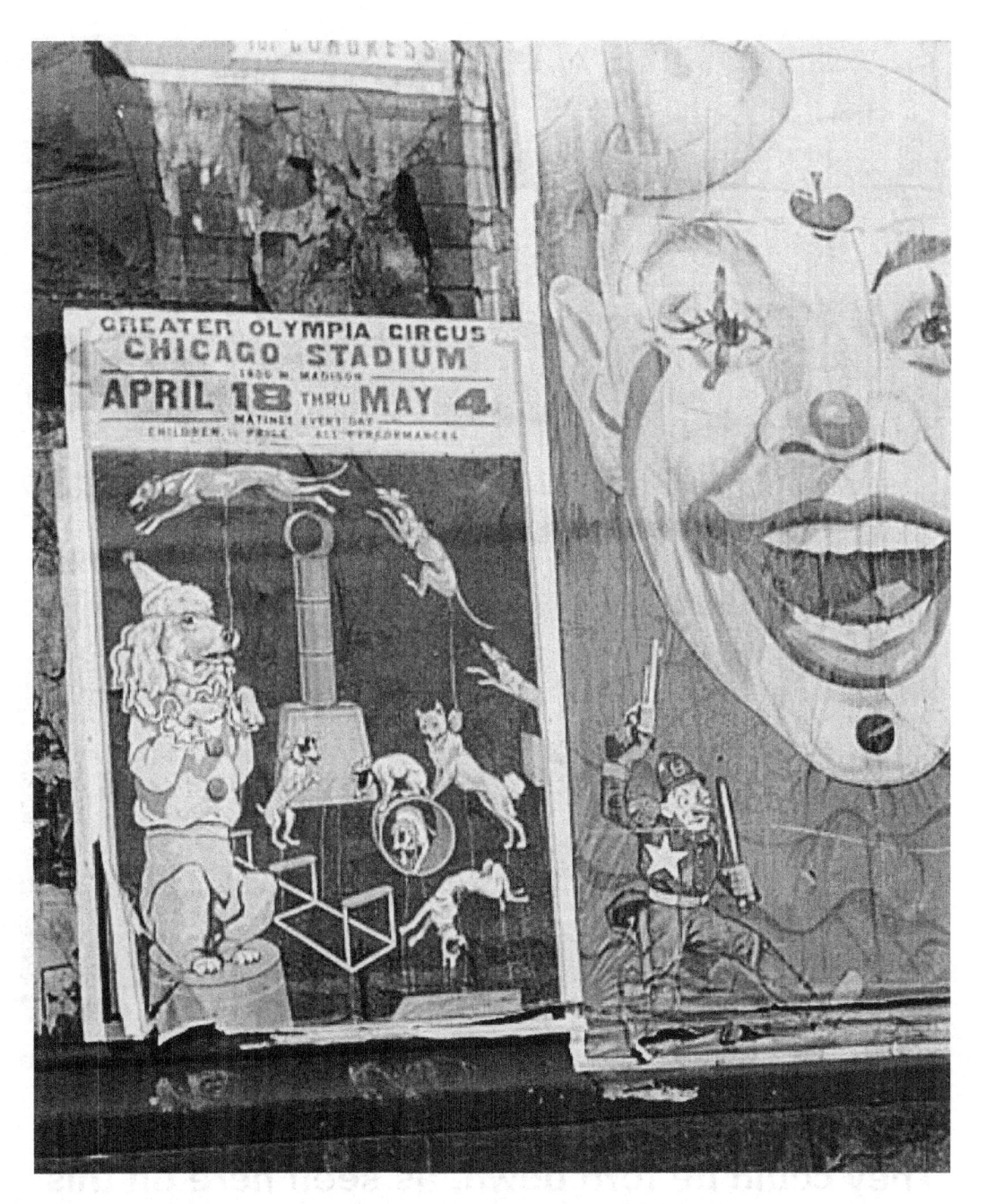

More circus posters, these in Chicago

Edwin Rosskam, Library of Congress

Illinois 1936

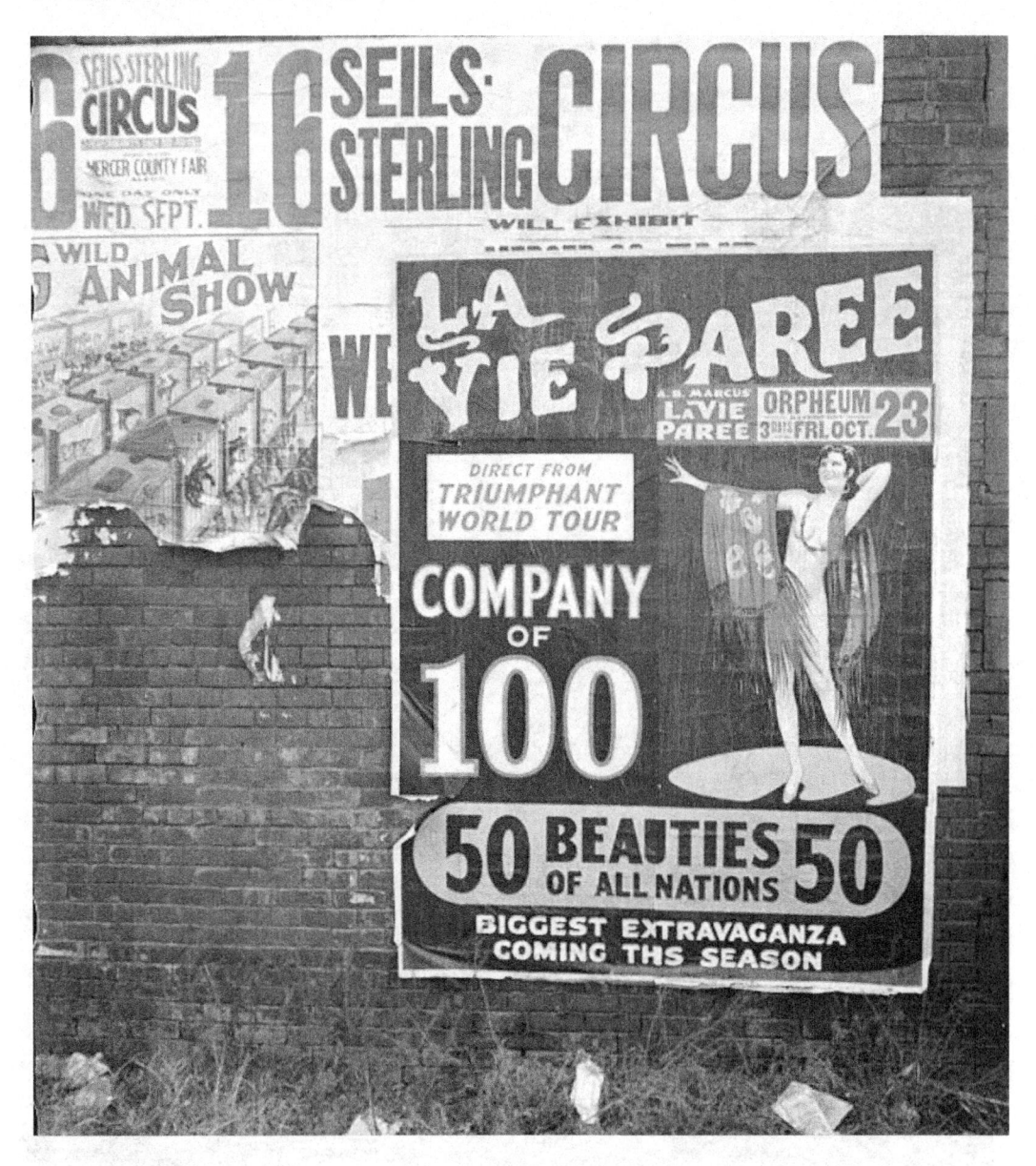

Posters weren't as permanent as painted ads: They could be torn down, as seen here on this building in Aledo, Illinois, west of Chicago

Ben Shahn, Library of Congress

Florida 1953

Sensational movies and adult offerings are advertised outside this theater in Jacksonville, next door to a palm reader

State Library and Archives of Florida

Tennessee 1935

Bills for Stud, Raleigh, and Twenty Grand cigarettes (named for a racehorse) are plastered on a wall in Nashville

Ben Shahn, Library of Congress

New York 1954

Bills are common outside theaters; these New York City posters were at the entrance of Hubert's Museum & Flea Circus, founded in 1925 on 42nd Street

Angelo Rizutto, Library of Congress

Pennsylvania 1913

Early billboards like these in Pittsburgh were often stacked to maximize the available space; Vin Fiz Sparkling Grape Drink (top) sponsored Calbraith Perry Rodgers' first transcontinental flight — in a Wright Brothers plane in 1911

University of Pittsburgh

SIGNPOST UP AHEAD, THE EAST

Pennsylvania 1913

Double-stacked billboards in Pittsburgh advertised Haig & Haig whisky, Puffed Rice or Wheat, a bill at the Hippodrome, and Prince Albert in a can (let him out!)

University of Pittsburgh

New York
1941

This small billboard nailed to a stick near Bridgeport, New York, functioned as both a road sign and an ad for the feed company that erected it

John Collier Jr., Library of Congress

Vermont 1941

"Last gas" signs such as this one north of Highgate Springs, likely on U.S. Highway 7 en route to the Canadian border functioned as both warnings and ads

Jack Delano, Library of Congress

Ohio 2018

A rotted, partially legible sign for some kind of shop east of Cairo, Ohio, on the Lincoln Highway

Stephen H. Provost

SIGNPOST UP AHEAD, THE EAST

Small temporary billboards like this one in Syracuse advertising ice cream have long been a staple of eateries and snack shops

John Collier Jr., Library of Congress

Ohio 1938

Some billboards are temporary "for sale" signs; this one advertising a farm to be sold at public auction appeared in New Carlisle, Ohio

Ben Shahn, Library of Congress

Florida 1966

During election season, politicians use billboards to promote their candidacy for public office, as Claude Kirk did in his successful bid for Florida governor in 1966

State Library and Archives of Florida

Pennsylvania

c. 1949

Fear and racism have often stoked political campaigns, as illustrated by this billboard in Pittsburgh featuring a pair of menacing clawed hands and a girl clutching a blackface doll

University of Pittsburgh

Michigan 1948

Future president Gerald R. Ford made his first bid for office in 1948, when he easily won election to the U.S. House of Representatives

National Archives

Pennsylvania
1935

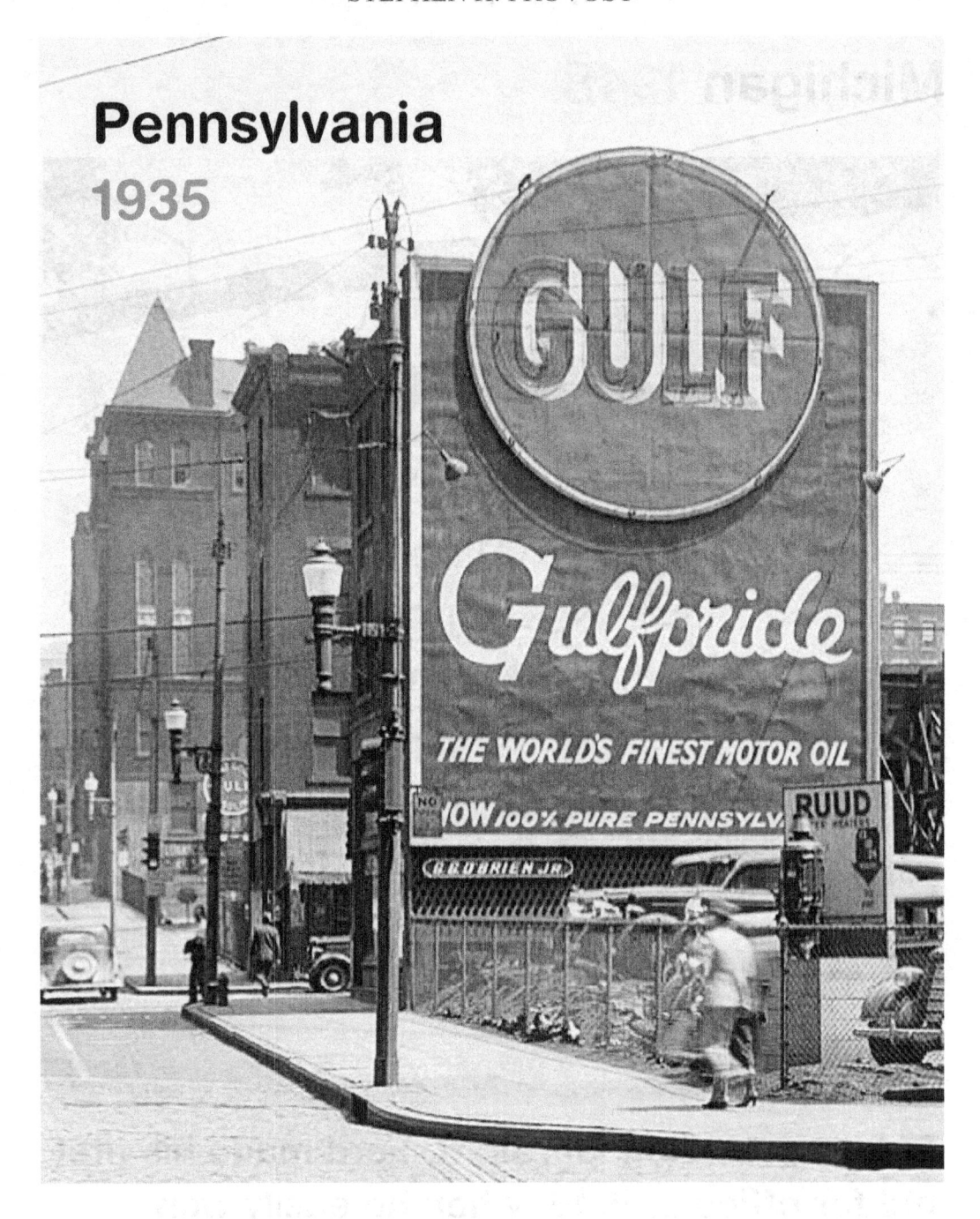

A Gulf Oil billboard on Bigelow Boulevard at Grant Street in Pittsburgh prepared drivers for a Gulf station a block farther on

University of Pittsburgh

Florida 1952

Billboards are sometimes used to promote businesses on site; this one could be seen at the Sunset Cove Tea Room in Key Largo

State Library and Archives of Florida

STEPHEN H. PROVOST

Maine 1984

Odd shapes can be an eye-catching feature of billboards like this one at Reed's Gifts in
Warren, Maine

John Margolies, Library of Congress

West Virginia 1920s

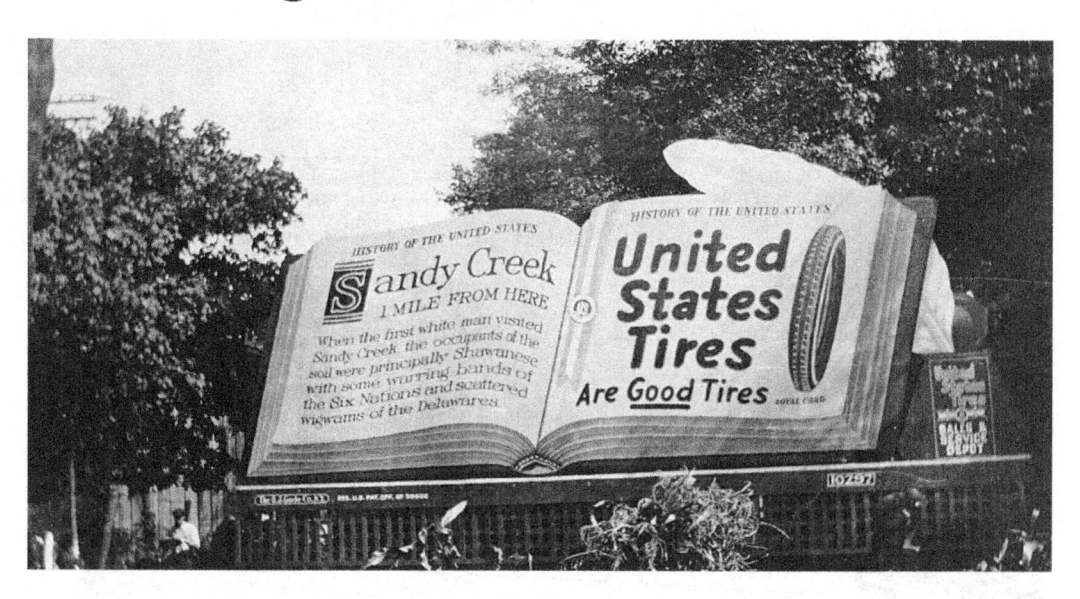

Pennsylvania 1920s

United States Tires, forerunner of Uniroyal, placed these signs at Sandy Creek (top), Pittsburgh, and across the country

University of Michigan Digital Archives

Indiana c. 1923

The Lincoln Highway Association put up this billboard to highlight the "Ideal Section" of the road near modern U.S. Highway 30 in Shererville, meant to highlight the benefits of traveling on paved highways

University of Michigan Digital Archives

Pennsylvania 1926

The high price of food was a selling point for Frigidaire in this billboard on the Boulevard of Allies west of Brady Street in Pittsburgh

University of Pittsburgh

Kentucky 1940

A liquor dispensary was a popular destination north of the Tennessee-Kentucky state line, where drivers entered a "wet" state from a "dry" jurisdiction

Marion Post Wolcott, Library of Congress

SIGNPOST UP AHEAD, THE EAST

Ohio 1940

Two locally brewed products put up signs in an Ohio cornfield: Buckeye Beer was Toledo's second-oldest business, dating back 1838, and Red Top Beer-Ale came from Cincinnati

Ben Shahn, Library of Congress

Michigan 1942

Imperial Whiskey was "velveted for smoothness," according to this sign on Cadillac Square in Detroit

Arthur S. Siegel, Library of Congress

District of Columbia 1940

Northampton Brewery in Pennsylvania wanted to make sure residents in the nation's capital never forgot its Tru-Blu Beer, which was bottled from 1933 until the brewery closed in 1950

Edward Rosskam, Library of Congress

Keystone Light beer is featured on a sign at a "Y" intersection on old Route 66 (current State Route 4) in Staunton, Illinois

Stephen H. Provost

No bull: This sign atop the Bull Durham plant at Blackwell and Pettigrew streets in Durham still lights up at night

Stephen H. Provost

North Carolina 2022

Another "bullboard" down the block on West Pettigrew Street in Durham dates from a time when you could "roll your own and save your roll" for just 5 cents

Stephen H. Provost

SIGNPOST UP AHEAD, THE EAST

New York 1918

Those attending a Red Cross parade down Fifth Avenue in New York City couldn't avoid seeing this billboard for Piedmont, "the Virginia cigarette" (just a nickel a pack!)

National Archives

New York 1943

This ad for Camel Cigarettes on Times Square in New York City was installed in 1941 and actually blew smoke for the next 26 years; you'd walk a mile to see it

John Vachon, Library of Congress

SIGNPOST UP AHEAD, THE EAST

Pennsylvania 1951

Armour Star pork sausage had a captive audience with this billboard, seen from Pittsburgh's William Penn Hotel at Sixth Avenue and Grant Street

University of Pittsburgh

New Jersey

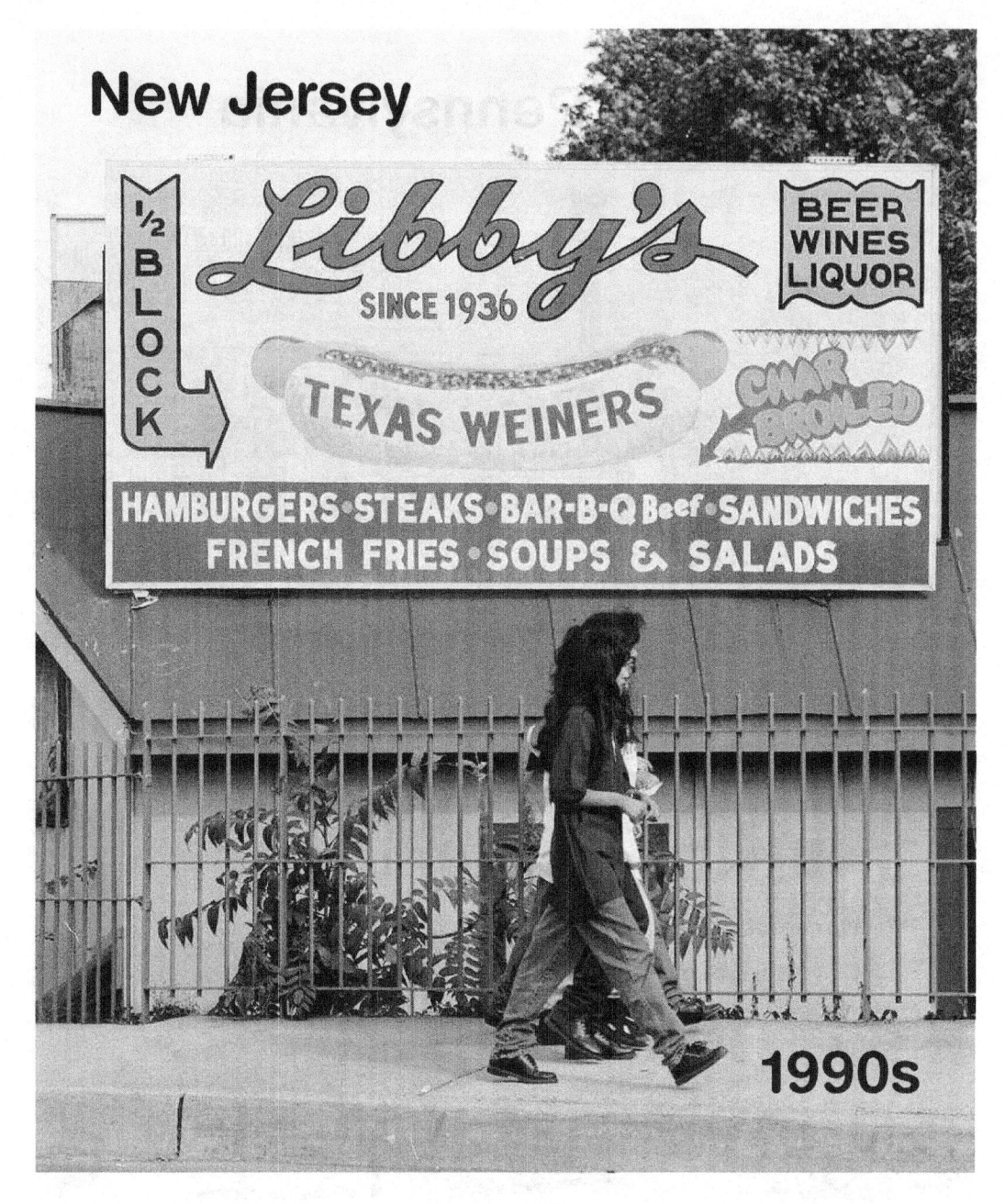

1990s

Libby's Restaurant wasn't in the Lone Star State, it was in Paterson, where it posted this sign at McBride and Wayne Avenues touting its "Texas weiners"

Paterson Project Collection, Library of Congress

The Roadside America Miniature Village sold gifts, hex signs — a form of Dutch folk art often found on barns — and souvenirs on U.S. Highway 22 in Shartlesville

John Margolies, Library of Congress

Florida c. 1950

Everybody was welcome at the "not private" Caribbean Club in Key Largo, where you could find "good food," hotel rooms, a bar, and boats

State Library and Archives of Florida

SIGNPOST UP AHEAD, THE EAST

Ohio 1938

An arrow-shaped billboard, possibly on U.S. Highway 40, pointed the way toward Buckeye Lake State Park east of Columbus and the Harbor Hills neighborhood on the lake's north shore

Ben Shahn, Library of Congress

STEPHEN H. PROVOST

Pennsylvania 1965

The new-model Ford Mustang and Johnny Carson's "Tonight Show" were featured in these downtown Pittsburgh billboards

University of Pittsburgh

Fireworks stands are common on this section of U.S. Highway 501 in South Carolina, just south of the North Carolina state line; this one in Dillon offers everything from Cherry Bombs to Black Cats

Stephen H. Provost

New York
1940

The VFW had this message for motorists in Buffalo shortly before the U.S. entered World War II: "Foreign 'isms' can't divide Americans"

Dixon Royden, Library of Congress

Pennsylvania 1950

Religious messages aren't uncommon by the highway, as this sign in Scottsdale, Pennsylvania indicates

Mennonite Church USA

North Carolina 2021

A religious billboard near the mountain town of Boone dwarfs a Citgo sign

Stephen H. Provost

North Carolina 2021

Kentucky coal miner and evangelist Harrison Hayes handcrafted dozens of concrete signs with messages like this one on U.S. Highway 70 in Mebane

Stephen H. Provost

Georgia 1939

A religious question (minus the question mark) shares space with signs for a fertilizer and Green Spot, an orange soft drink, in Greene County

Marion Post Wolcott, Library of Congress

Illinois 2018

This Burma Shave rhyming series was found along Route 66

Stephen H. Provost

(Continued on next page)

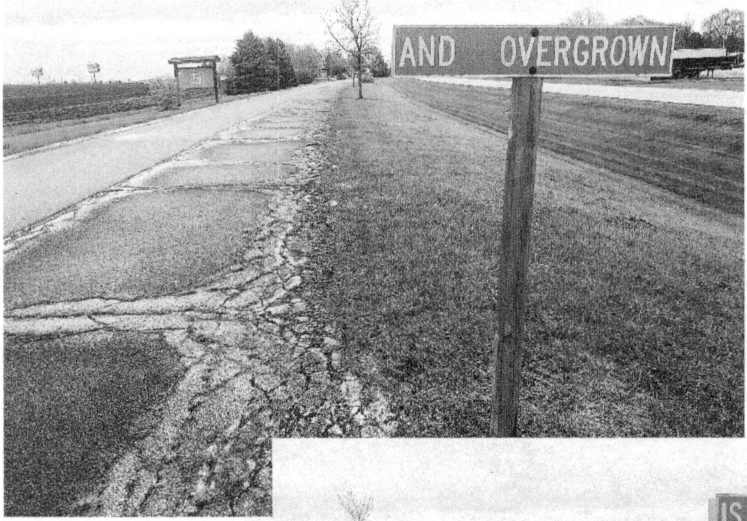
AND OVERGROWN

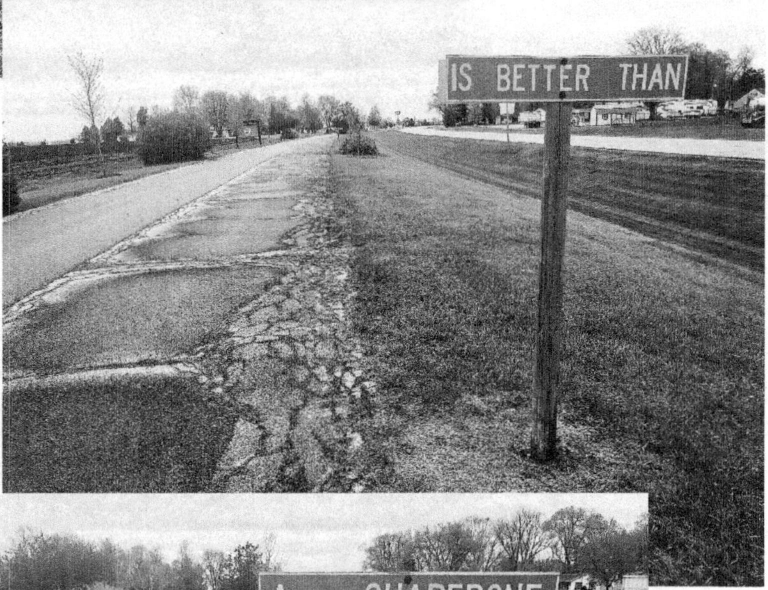
IS BETTER THAN

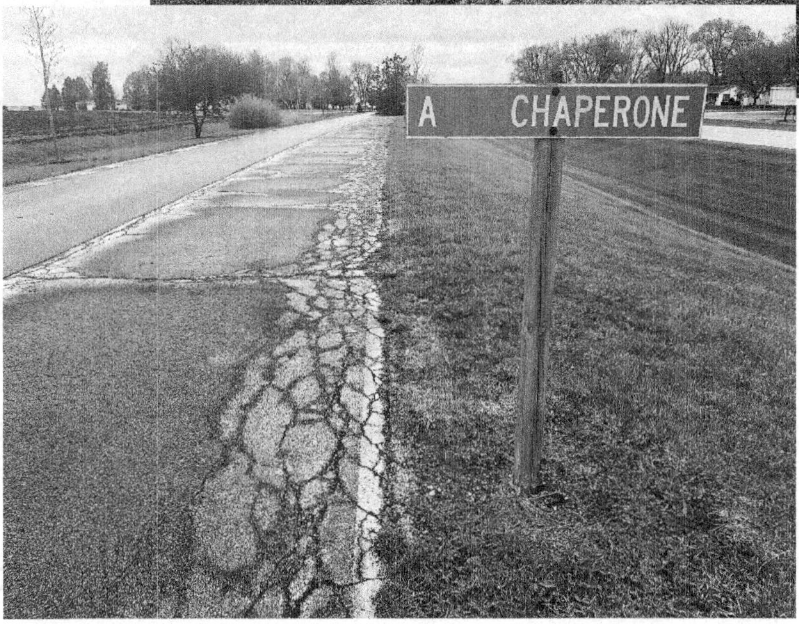
A CHAPERONE

Kentucky 2021

Big Mike's Rock & Gift Shop flags down travelers to Mammoth Cave in Kentucky

Stephen H. Provost

North Carolina 1937

The AAA-approved Hotel Carolina was "Raleigh's newest" hotel when this photo was taken, featuring a radio and a fan in each room; you could stay there for $2.50 a night

State Archives of North Carolina

SIGNPOST UP AHEAD, THE EAST

A billboard boasting "the world's highest standard of living" seems out of place in a less-than-prosperous section of Birmingham

Arthur Rothstein, Library of Congress

**West Virginia
1937**

The same anti-Depression sign campaign shared space with a Coca-Cola ad in another impoverished area, near Kingwood

Edwin Locke, Library of Congress

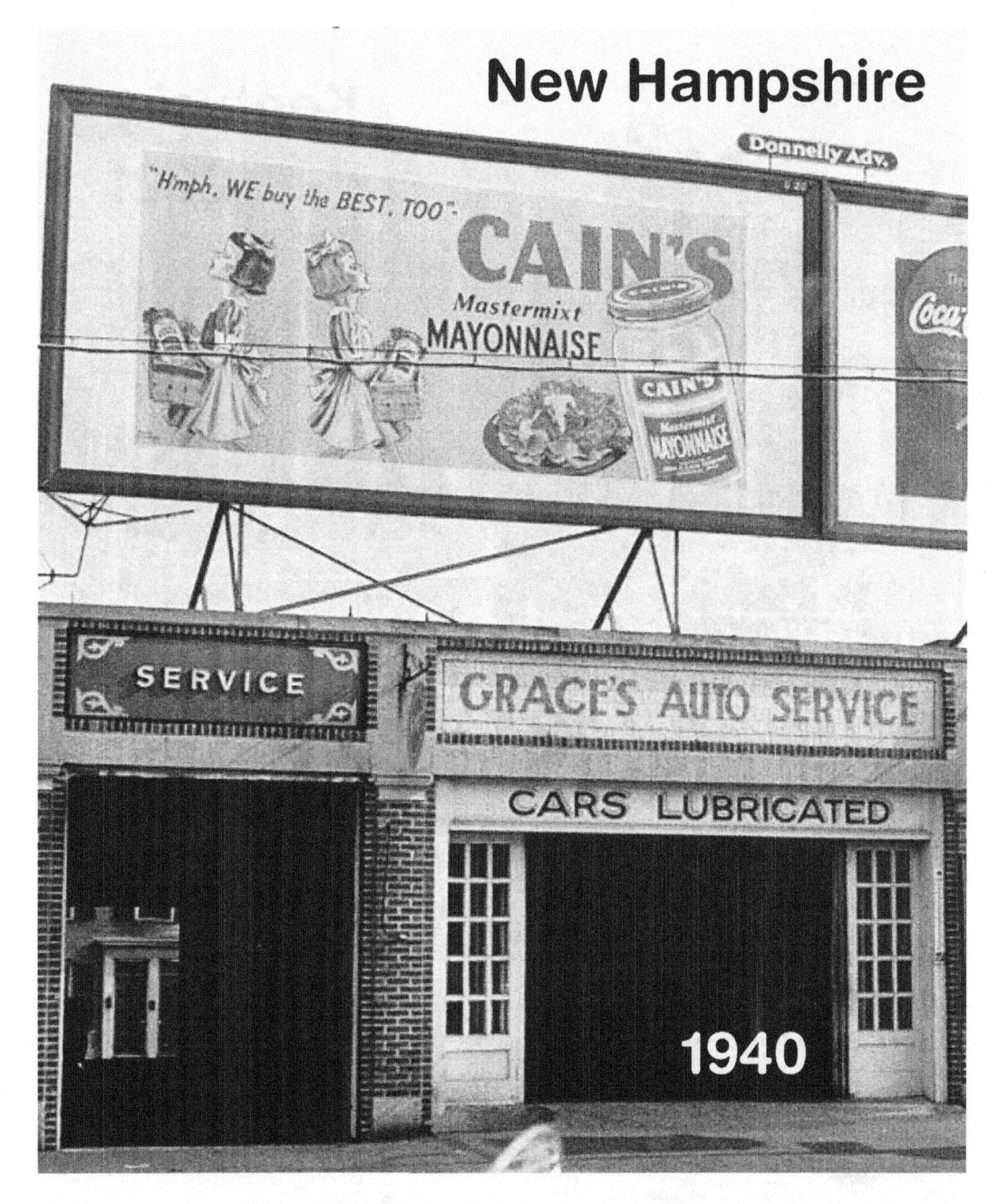

Cain's started out in 1914 as a Boston-based cheese distributor and advertised its Mastermixt Mayonnaise on this billboard in the coastal city of Portsmouth

Walter Payton, Library of Congress

Onyx Cave is a tourist attraction off State Route 70 **in Kentucky near Cave City**

Stephen H. Provost

SIGNPOST UP AHEAD, THE EAST

Georgia 1936

A pair of movies — "Chatterbox," starring Anne Shirley, and the Carole Lombard vehicle "Love Before Breakfast" get the star treatment on these Atlanta billboards

Walker Evans, Library of Congress

North Carolina

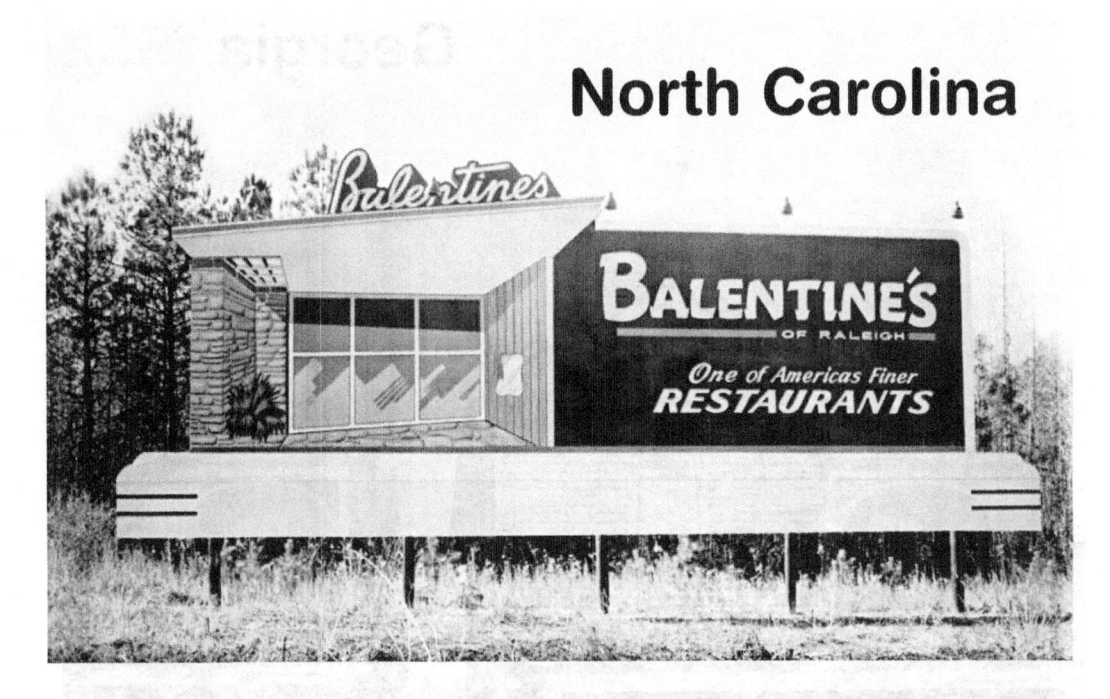

c. 1960s

A billboard seen during daytime and at night promotes Balentine's Cafeteria in Raleigh, open from 1960 to 1999

Albert Barden, State Archives of North Carolina

Virginia 1954

Hey, Virginia drivers, fresh up with 7UP; so says this sign on Belvidere Street (U.S. Highway 301) just north of the Lee Bridge in Richmond

Adolph B. Rice, Library of Virginia

Indiana 1937

Boone's Pharmacy in Kentland advertised fountain service and "medicinal liquors"

John Vachon, Library of Congress

Some billboards remain standing long after they've been abandoned; this one off U.S. Highway 30 near Middle Point referred to a restaurant and color T.V., but little else remains legible

Stephen H. Provost

Nebraska 1938

Cities such as Lincoln, Nebraska's state capital, used billboards like this one by Robinson Inc. to bolster civic pride, urging local residents to "say a good word for Lincoln"

John Vachon, Library of Congress

SIGNPOST UP AHEAD, THE EAST

Maryland 1940

This double billboard on U.S. Highway 1 near Laurel, Maryland, gave motorists a choice between Maryland, where there was "so much to see" and the New Castle Ferry to New York

Jack Delano, Library of Congress

Wheeler's Fast Service Laundry & Dry Cleaning on Brandon Avenue, between U.S. Highways 220 and 221, has been in business in Roanoke since 1950

Stephen H. Provost

SIGNPOST UP AHEAD, THE EAST

North Carolina 1949

Smith-Melville Dairy bought space atop this building at Wilmington and Morgan streets in Raleigh to promote its milk; Melville Dairy of Burlington bought the Smith Dairy of Raleigh in 1948

State Archives of North Carolina

STEPHEN H. PROVOST

Pennsylvania 1936

Visitors to the Terminal Theatre at 69th and Market in Upper Darby were treated to this billboard for Atlantic's White Flash gasoline

Paul Vanderbilt, Wikimedia Commons

IV
Guideposts:
This Way, That Far

Multiple signs on U.S. Highway 11, the Lee Highway through Abingdon, point the way to various highway options near the center of town

Stephen H. Provost

Maryland

Rates of Toll
on the Cumberland Road in Maryland

Horse and rider	5¢
1-Horse carriage	10¢
2-Horse carriage	15¢
2-Horse wagon	25¢
each additional horse	5¢
2-Passenger automobile	20¢
5-Passenger automobile	25¢
7-Passenger automobile	30¢
Motor Trucks	
1-Ton	25¢
2-Ton	30¢
3-Ton	35¢
4-Ton	40¢
5-Ton	40¢
Over 5 Ton	50¢

Rates are posted in this undated photo for the Cumberland Toll Road in Maryland, the nation's first major improved highway

National Archives

Ohio-Indiana
1920s

A sign marks the Ohio-Indiana state line along the Lincoln Highway, the nation's first transcontinental road

University of Michigan Library Digital Archives

Illinois 2018

Famed Route 66 begins at this point in Chicago and heads southwest to Santa Monica, California

Stephen H. Provost

STEPHEN H. PROVOST

North Carolina 2020

A purple gorilla and a statue of Jesus watch traffic pass by on the rural Donna Fargo Highway in North Carolina

Stephen H. Provost

SIGNPOST UP AHEAD, THE EAST

Pennsylvania Avenue, **site of the White House, was designated as DC 4, an extension of Maryland Route 4, in the mid-20th century**

John Ferrell, Library of Congress

STEPHEN H. PROVOST

Pennsylvania 1921

A detour sign posted by the Pennsylvania State Highway Department along the Lincoln Highway at Gettysburg directs traffic to Pittsburgh

University of Michigan Library Digital Archives

South Carolina 2021

A stop sign and highway shields guard the junction of U.S. Routes 1 and 52 just outside the small town of Cheraw

Stephen H. Provost

Stop signs were originally painted yellow, like other hazard signs; this one was on Columbia Island in Arlington, just south of Washington, D.C.

National Archives

Alabama 1951

Black-on-white shields were adopted with the creation of the federal highway system in 1926; U.S. highways 11 and 43 shared this stretch of road near Eutaw, Alabama

T.W. Kines, National Archives

Virginia 1951

This section of road in U.S. Highway 1 and its auxiliary route, U.S. 301, are co-signed in front of a private residence in Virginia

T.W. Kines, National Archives

SIGNPOST UP AHEAD, THE EAST

North Carolina 2022

Drivers on U.S. Business 70 in Durham could choose several routes, including U.S. 15, U.S. 501, and Interstate 85

Stephen H. Provost

Mississippi 1951

This bypass for U.S. highways 80 and 11 let drivers skirt central Meridian, Mississippi; note the white concrete and single, unbroken dark line

T.W. Kines, National Archives

Florida 1946

A Florida Highway Patrol officer changes a couple's tire on a road cosigned as U.S. highways 17 and 92, as well as State Route 600 in Central Florida

State Library and Archives of Florida

City streets are often named after famous residents; this one in Danville is named for Lady Astor, who was born there but later became the first woman seated in the British Parliament

Stephen H. Provost

Pennsylvania 1920s

This Lincoln Highway road sign was maintained by the Duquesne Light Service

University of Michigan Library Digital Archives

Old-style obelisk street signs were used in this Huntington neighborhood

Stephen H. Provost

North Carolina 1920s

A wrecked car sits abandoned beside a sign for U.S. Route 311 in North Carolina; the route follows several different highways for 62 miles from Winston-Salem to Danville, Virginia

State Archives of North Carolina

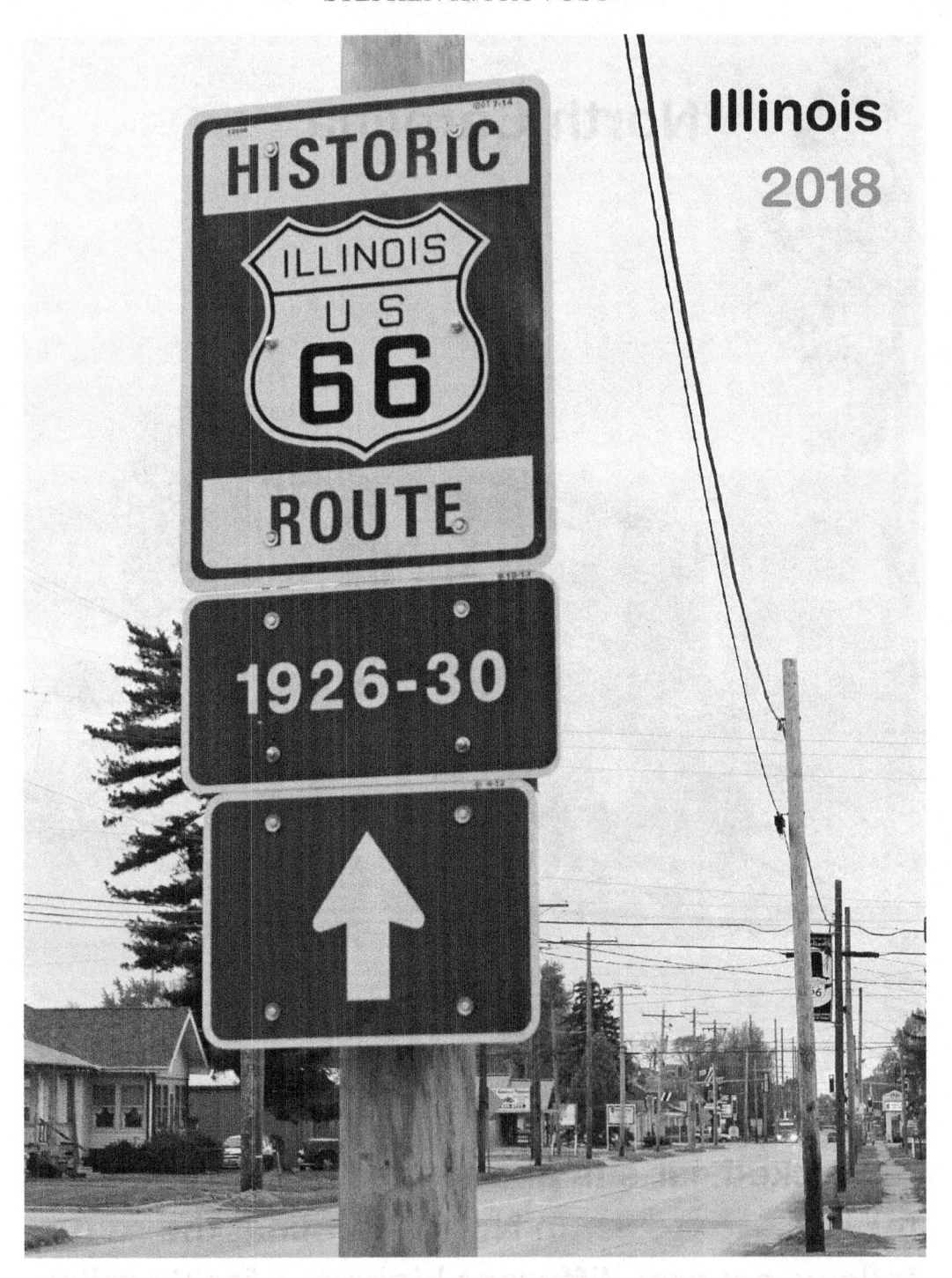

A historic marker in Carlinville shows the path Route 66 took through town from 1926 to 1930

Stephen H. Provost

Pennsylvania 2018

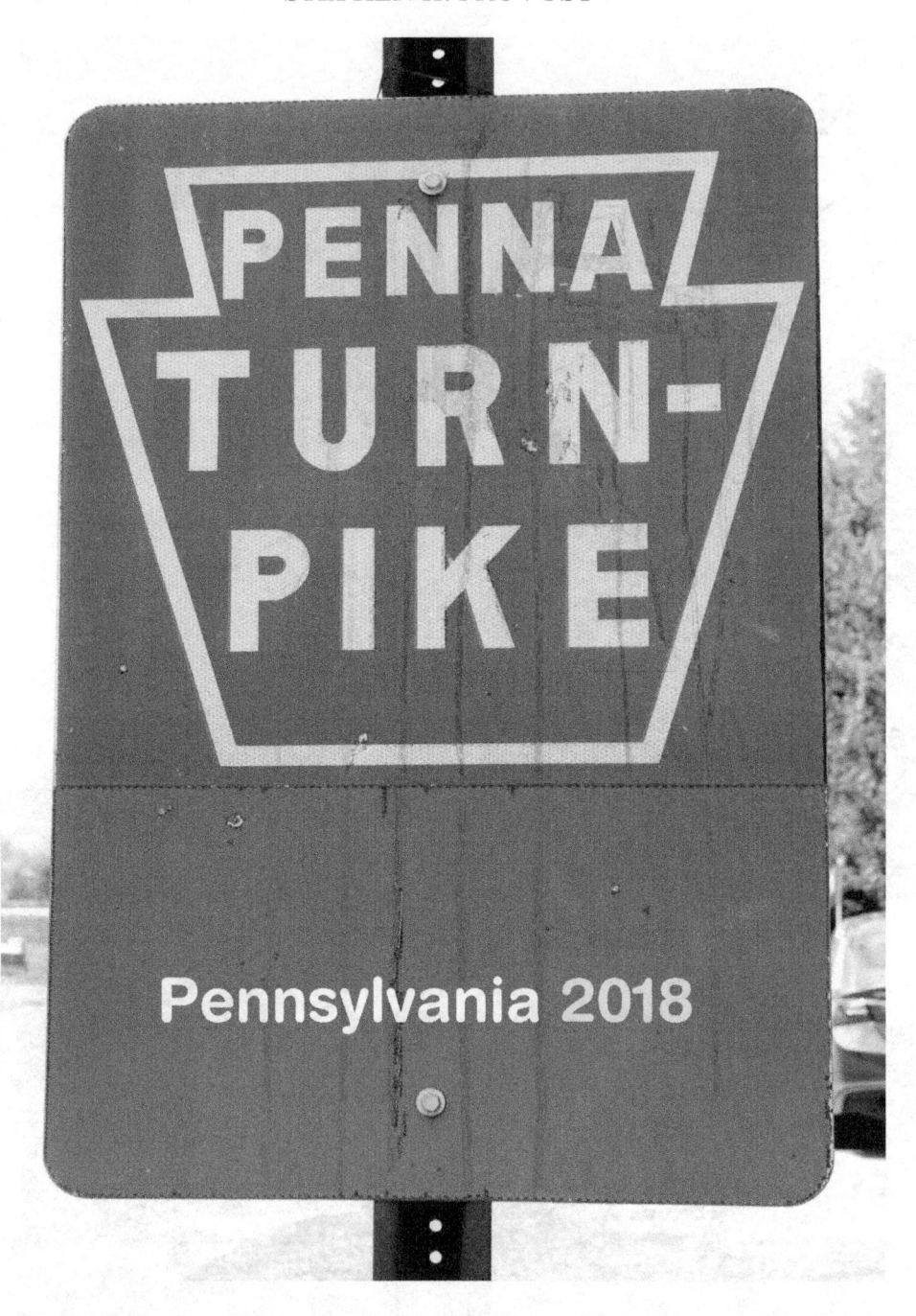

The Pennsylvania Turnpike is an east-west toll road that runs from the Philadelphia area west to Pittsburgh and connects to the Ohio Turnpike

Stephen H. Provost

Delaware 1952

Overhead signs were meant to be visible from farther down the road; this one directs drivers left to U.S. Highway 13 through Philadelphia and Wilmington or right to U.S. 40 and the Delaware Memorial Bridge

T.W. Kines, National Archives

An overhead sign on 5th Avenue at U.S. 60 offers directions to Point Pleasant (home of the legendary Mothman), Barboursville, and Proctorville via Ohio Route 7

Stephen H. Provost

Virginia 1943

Signs point the way to U.S. 50 and 29 via the Memorial Bridge and U.S. 1 via the 14th Street Bridge at the Pentagon

H. Ritter, National Archives

Massachusetts 1973

This photo shows Route C1 (City Route 1), an alternate route of U.S. Highway 1 in downtown Boston, at the junction of U.S. 1 and State Route 145 to Winthrop

Philip Manheim, National Archives

Maryland 1977

A speed limit sign on the Capital Beltway was changed for this photo to reflect the national 55 mph maximum adopted in 1974 to conserve fuel and repealed in 1995

Warren K. Leffler, Library of Congress

New York 1954

Motorists traveling on U.S. Route 9 through Yonkers were expected to observe a speed limit of 20 mph in 1954

Angelo Rizzuto, Library of Congress

Illinois 1939

The speed limit was 45 miles per hour on the U.S. Highway 12 city route through Chicago

Arthur Rothstein, Library of Congress

SIGNPOST UP AHEAD, THE EAST

New York   1938

New York Route 1A ran 18 miles through New York City from the Holland Tunnel north to U.S. 1; it existed from 1934 to the early 1960s

T.W. Kines, National Archives

STEPHEN H. PROVOST

New York
1941

WE LOVE OUR CHILDREN. DRIVE SLOW.

Neighborhoods like this one in Utica have been protecting kids at play for years

Arthur Rothstein, Library of Congress

Connecticut 1949

It isn't a speed trap if you put up a sign, as Connecticut state police did on this section of State Route 15 in Glastonbury, just outside Hartford, heading south toward New Haven

Tullio Saba

Vermont 1939

Warning lights greet motorists at a railroad crossing in Shaftsbury

Russell Lee, Library of Congress

SIGNPOST UP AHEAD, THE EAST

Ohio 1939

A more primitive railroad crossing sign in Atlanta, Ohio, warned of "danger" but didn't come equipped with lights or crossing arm

Arthur Rothstein, Library of Congress

STEPHEN H. PROVOST

West Virginia 1935

A Bell System public phone was available on this highway corner in Reedsville

Walker Evans, Library of Congress

SIGNPOST UP AHEAD, THE EAST

Maryland 1959

Using a public phone was easy on Route 40 north of Baltimore, where you could drive up and place a call without even leaving your seat

Warren K. Leffler, Library of Congress

STEPHEN H. PROVOST

Ohio 1924

A steep grade lay ahead on this section of the Lincoln Highway in Ohio

University of Michigan Library Digital Archives

Florida 1994

Gators apparently get their own crosswalks in Lee County, if this sign is to be believed

State Library and Archives of Florida

STEPHEN H. PROVOST

North Carolina 1950

Pauls Gap, aka Polls Gap, is marked by a wooden sign along Heintooga Ridge Road in western North Carolina

T.W. Kines, National Archives

SIGNPOST UP AHEAD, THE EAST

Tennessee 1939

Striking copper miners put their own sign up under mileage signs on Tennessee Route 68 **at Ducktown**

Marion Post Wolcott, Library of Congress

STEPHEN H. PROVOST

North Carolina 1927

Mileage markers in Williamston all point in the same direction

Surry Parker Collection, State Archives of North Carolina

SIGNPOST UP AHEAD, THE EAST

Florida
1960s

A road sign along the Florida coast directs drivers (and sunbathers) to Hollywood, Miami, and nearby Fort Lauderdale

State Library and Archives of Florida

South Carolina 1941

Road signs at a crossroad near the Santee-Cooper Basin show mileage to WPA camps and declare that Cross's Cross Road "will not be inundated or affected"

Jack Delano, Library of Congress

SIGNPOST UP AHEAD, THE EAST

Tennessee
1937

ROCKWOOD 24
KINGSTON 36
HARRIMAN 37
KNOXVILLE 75
CHATTANOOGA 98
HOMESTEAD 4
PIKEVILLE 31
DUNLAP 52
CHATTANOOGA 87

A sign in an intersection at Crossville, between Nashville and Knoxville, offered drivers plenty of options and information

Arthur Rothstein, Library of Congress

North Carolina
1950

A directional sign on the Blue Ridge Parkway at U.S. Highway 21 shows the distance to Roaring Gap and Sparta, together with those towns' amenities

T.W. Kines, National Archives

V
You've Arrived

North Carolina 2022

Speaking of the Blue Ridge Parkway, here's a sign at the edge of Asheville marking the entrance to the 469-mile road from Virginia's Shenandoah Valley to North Carolina's Great Smoky Mountains National Park

Stephen H. Provost

Florida 1940

Ocala National Forest on State Road 500 in Florida, the oldest national forest east of the Mississippi River, was established in 1908

Edwin G. Thurlow, National Archives

SIGNPOST UP AHEAD, THE EAST

Illinois 1939

Local businesses including a drugstore, tavern, and funeral home joined forces with the local Lions Club to show motorists what they could expect in Hurst, a small town southwest of St. Louis along State Route 149

Arthur Rothstein, Library of Congress

Florida 1921

A giant likeness of Jack Tigertail, a leader in the Seminole community, welcomed tourists to Hialeah (spelled out phonetically) on what would become U.S. 27 at Hialeah Drive

State Library and Archives of Florida

North Carolina 2022

A sign in Durham highlights the history of "Black Wall Street," an area of successful Black-owned businesses along Parrish Street

Stephen H. Provost

Virginia 2020

If you're at Bassett Corporate Headquarters, you know you're in the town of Bassett, named after the famous furniture company

Stephen H. Provost

Bath, a coastal suburb of Portland along U.S. Highway 1 in southeast Maine, became popular with travelers who came to see its 19th-century architecture

Jack Delano, Library of Congress

Florida 1937

Not all welcome signs were two-dimensional — take, for instance, this stone highway marker, which greeted travelers in Polk County, central Florida

Jack Delano, Library of Congress

Virginia 2021

Water towers such as this one on U.S. 29 in Danville often provide a sense of place

Stephen H. Provost

West Virginia 2022

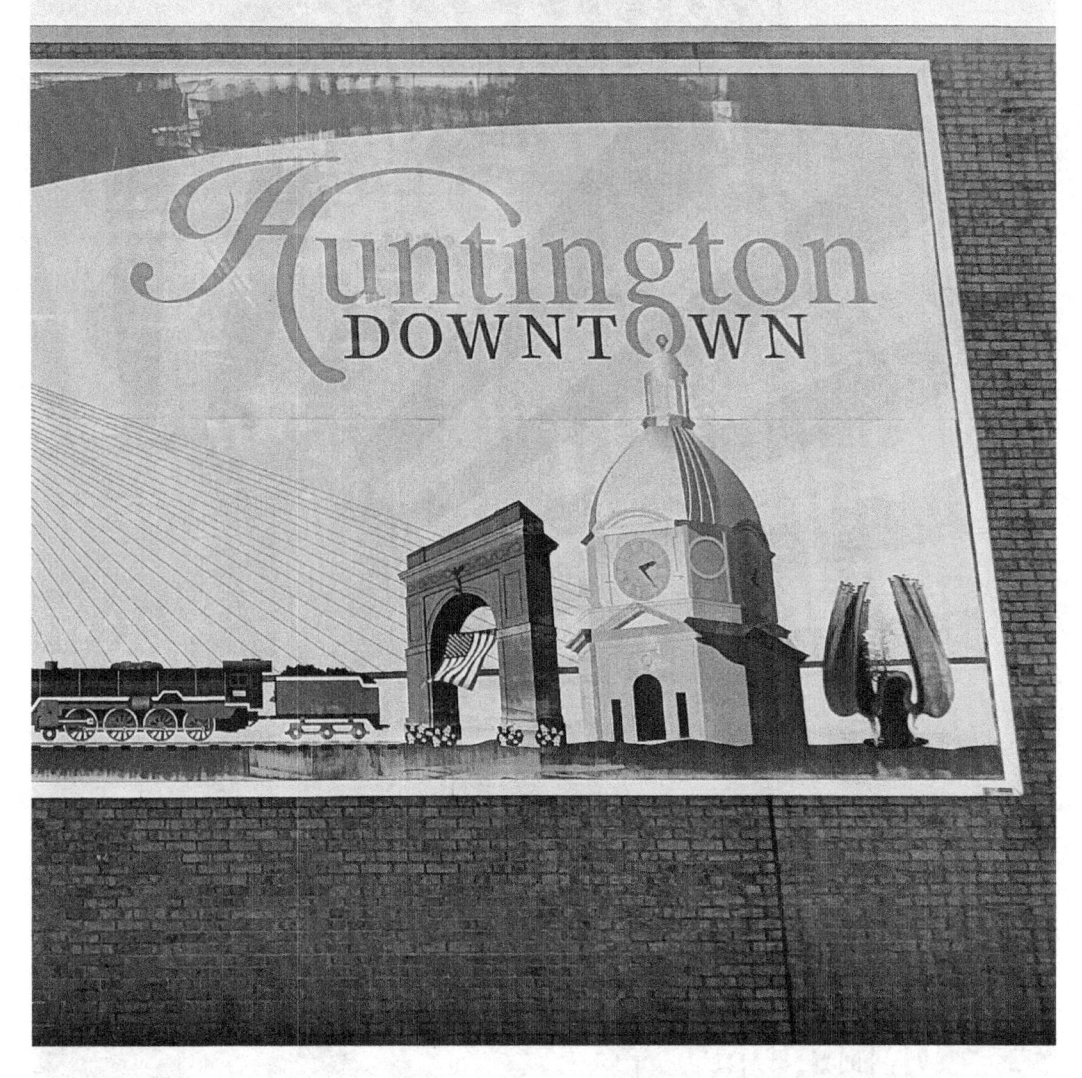

A mural on the back of a building informs visitors they're in downtown Huntington on the Ohio River, the state's second-largest city and the nation's second-busiest inland port

Stephen H. Provost

Florida 1947

A family enjoying the postwar travel boom stops to look for directions beside a billboard welcoming visitors to Florida

State Library and Archives of Florida

A vinyl sign affixed to a lamppost in Uptown Martinsville carries the town slogan, "A City Without Limits"

Stephen H. Provost

Indiana 1937

Signs on U.S. Highway 52 direct motorists to Swihart's Garage and downtown Kentland, a small town just east of the Illinois state line where the highway intersected with U.S. 41

John Vachon, Library of Congress

Ontario 1992

Stirling, a Canadian village two hours east of Toronto and just north of Lake Ontario, was "the little village with the big heart"; it would merge with the township of Rawdon in 1998

John Vachon, Library of Congress

1935

West Virginia

LIBERTY UNINCORPORATED

The speed limit was 25 through Liberty, an unincorporated community that lay north of Charleston on State Route 34 between U.S. 35 and modern Interstate 77

Ben Shahn, Library of Congress

STEPHEN H. PROVOST

Pennsylvania 1937

A stone obelisk marked both the Pennsylvania-Maryland State line and the Mason-Dixon Line five miles from Greencastle Borough in Pennsylvania on U.S. Highway 11

Ben Shahn, Library of Congress

The bi-state town of Bristol is "a good place to live" according to this Main Street sign at the Tennessee state line that was built in 1910 and originally stood atop a hardware store in town

Stephen H. Provost

It was typical for young women in swimsuits to tout Florida tourism, Potato Queen Peggy Davis did in this 1947 photo at Hastings, "the potato capital" on the state's northeast coast

State Library and Archives of Florida

SIGNPOST UP AHEAD, THE EAST

North Carolina

2022

You can't miss the fact that you're entering Greensboro, thanks to this water tower emblazoned with the city's name just off Interstate 73

Stephen H. Provost

Virginia 2022

Work on the Blue Ridge Parkway, considered by many one of the nation's most scenic drives, began in 1935 and was completed in the mid-1950s; this sign marks an entrance near Roanoke

Stephen H. Provost

A sign on Jefferson Street, just off U.S. 220 entering Roanoke tells a bit of the town's history

Stephen H. Provost

VI

Lighting Up the Night

STEPHEN H. PROVOST

Florida
1930

The 1,000-seat State Theatre on East Flagler Street in Miami opened as the Marco in 1910 and became the Fotosho four years later before reopening as the State in 1930

State Library and Archives of Florida

A neon billboard for Budweiser, the "king of bottled beer," dominates Times Square in New York City

The other half of the photo on the previous page shows lighted billboards for Chevrolet, Squibb Dental Cream, and Camel Cigarettes

Library of Congress

New York 1953

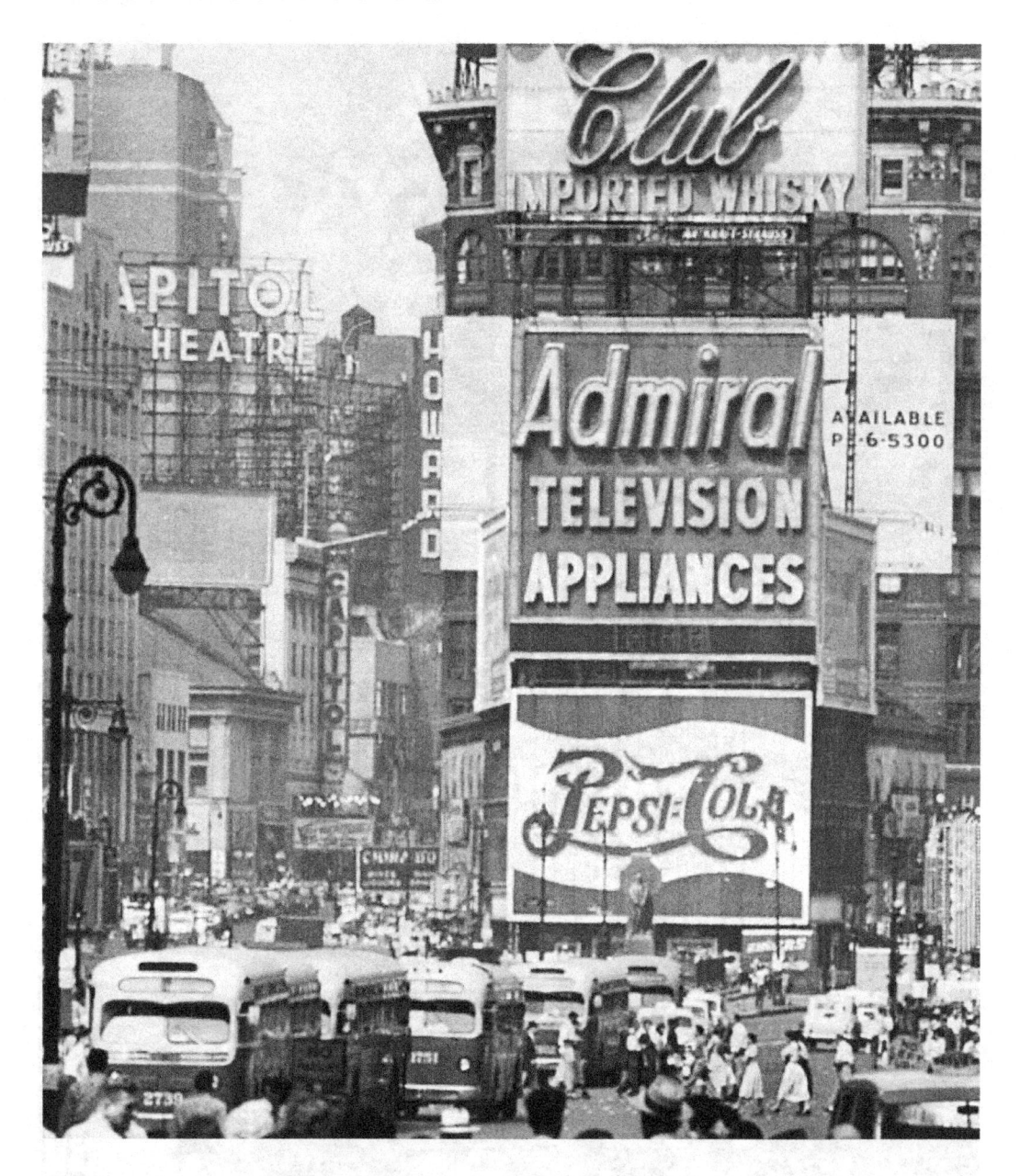

Nearly two decades later, this view of Times Square featured lighted billboards for Pepsi, Admiral appliances and imported whisky

Angelo Rizzuto, Library of Congress

STEPHEN H. PROVOST

New York 1953

Former heavyweight champ Jack Dempsey owned this bar on Times Square

Angelo Rizzuto, Library of Congress

SIGNPOST UP AHEAD, THE EAST

New York 1937

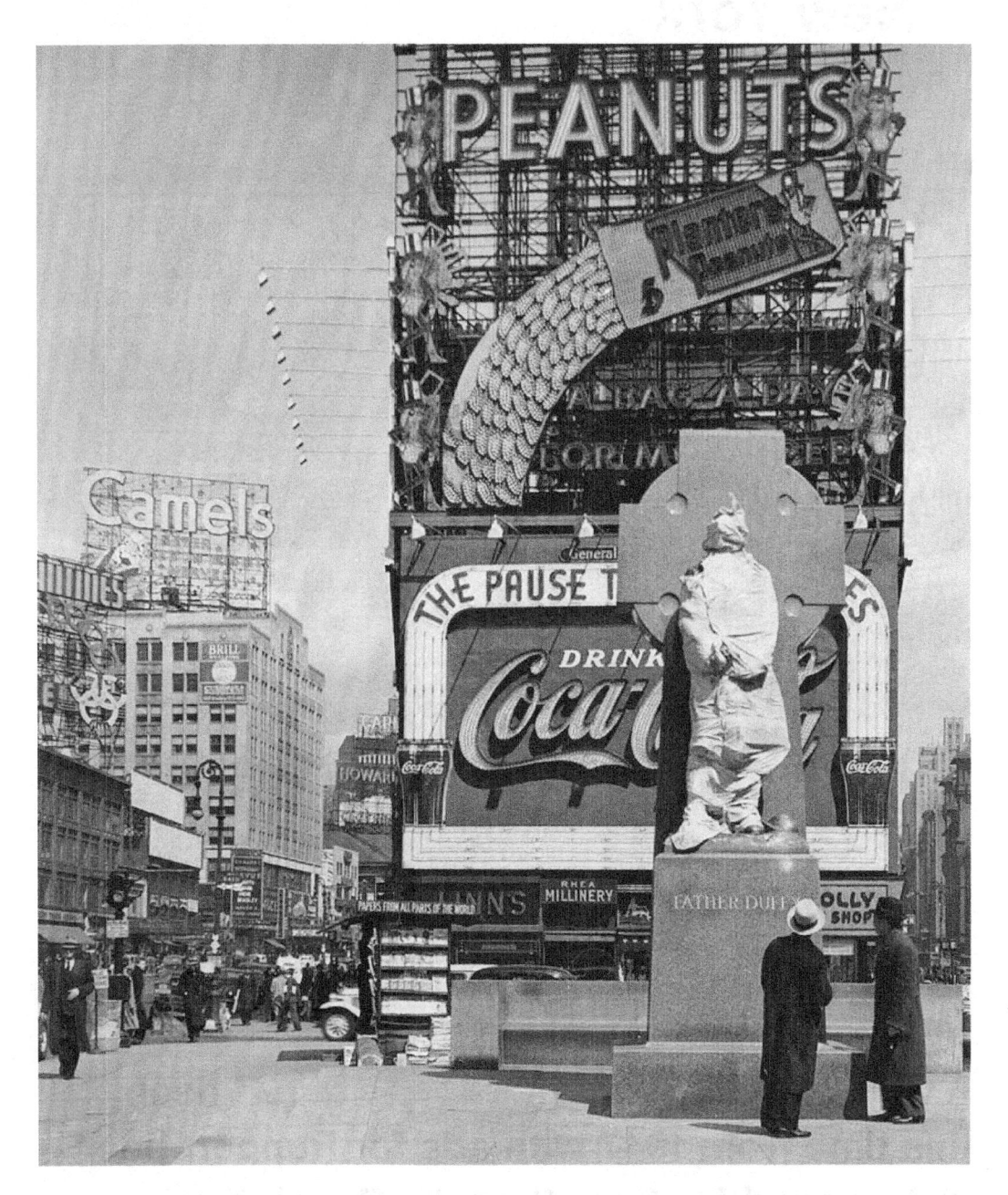

Planters Peanuts and Coca-Cola had neon Times Square billboards behind a statue of Father Francis P. Duffy

Peter Sekaer, Library of Congress

New York 1947

A view of the abundant Times Square neon, this time from 1947 with ads for Ruppert beer ("slow aged for finer flavor"), Pepsi, Kinsey Blended Whiskey, and Joan Crawford starring with Van Heflin in "Possessed."

William P. Gottlieb, Library of Congress

SIGNPOST UP AHEAD, THE EAST

Ohio 1975

A lighted motel sign advertising $10 rooms overlooks a Sunoco station in Cincinnati

National Archives

North Carolina
1947

The Ambassador on Fayetteville Street in Raleigh opened in 1928 and, in 1947, featured Lucille Ball and Boris Karloff in "Lured"

State Archives of North Carolina

New York 1946

The Apollo on West 125th Street in Harlem debuted in 1913 and was opened to Black patrons for the first time in 1934, becoming a venue for African-American performers

William P. Gottlieb, Library of Congress

STEPHEN H. PROVOST

Massachusetts 1963

The Publix, Paramount, and State theaters are pictured in this photo of Boston's commercial district

William P. Gottlieb, Library of Congress

SIGNPOST UP AHEAD, THE EAST

Illinois 2018

The nearly 4,000-seat Chicago Theatre on State Street opened in 1921

Stephen H. Provost

STEPHEN H. PROVOST

Florida 1964

The Florida Theatre's neon sign burns bright on Forsyth Street in downtown Jacksonville, where the nearly 2,000-seat venue opened in April of 1927

State Library and Archives of Florida

The Bristol on Main Street in Bristol, Tennessee, opened in 1931

Stephen H. Provost

STEPHEN H. PROVOST

Tennessee
2022

The Tennessee Theatre on South Gay Street in Knoxville made its debut in 1928

Stephen H. Provost

SIGNPOST UP AHEAD, THE EAST

New York 1958

TWA's lighted billboard at 43rd and Broadway in the Big Apple featured a model airplane

Andrew Rizzuto, Library of Congress

Pennsylvania 1984

Small-town America has its share of neon too, as well as distinctive signs like this one at Farmers Dairy in Hazelton — no bull!

John Margolies, Library of Congress

North Carolina

Doggin' it at Dick's Drive-In on Washington Street in the old downtown Leaksville area of Eden; it's been "the place to be since '63"

Stephen H. Provost

Delaware 1984

Delaware Auto Court on State Road in Rehoboth Beach offered efficiency apartments by the time this photo was taken in 1984

John Margolies, Library of Congress

Neon points travelers to the Fountain Motel on U.S. 29 in Rustburg, just south of Lynchburg

Stephen H. Provost

Florida 1946

Betty's Restaurant in Miami had enough electricity to power its neon sign as well as a big selling point during muggy Florida summers: air conditioning

State Library and Archives of Florida

Glen Echo Park in Bethesda — seen here with its giant neon gate sign — opened in the early 1900s, when many amusement parks were trolley-line destinations, and closed in 1968; it was the D.C. area's premier fun park

Ara Mesrobian, Library of Congress

West Virginia

2022

A brightly lit clown told visitors they'd arrived at Camden Park, off U.S. Highway 60 west of Huntington; one of just 13 end-of-the-trolley-line amusement parks left in the U.S. as of 2023, it opened in 1903

Stephen H. Provost

North Carolina

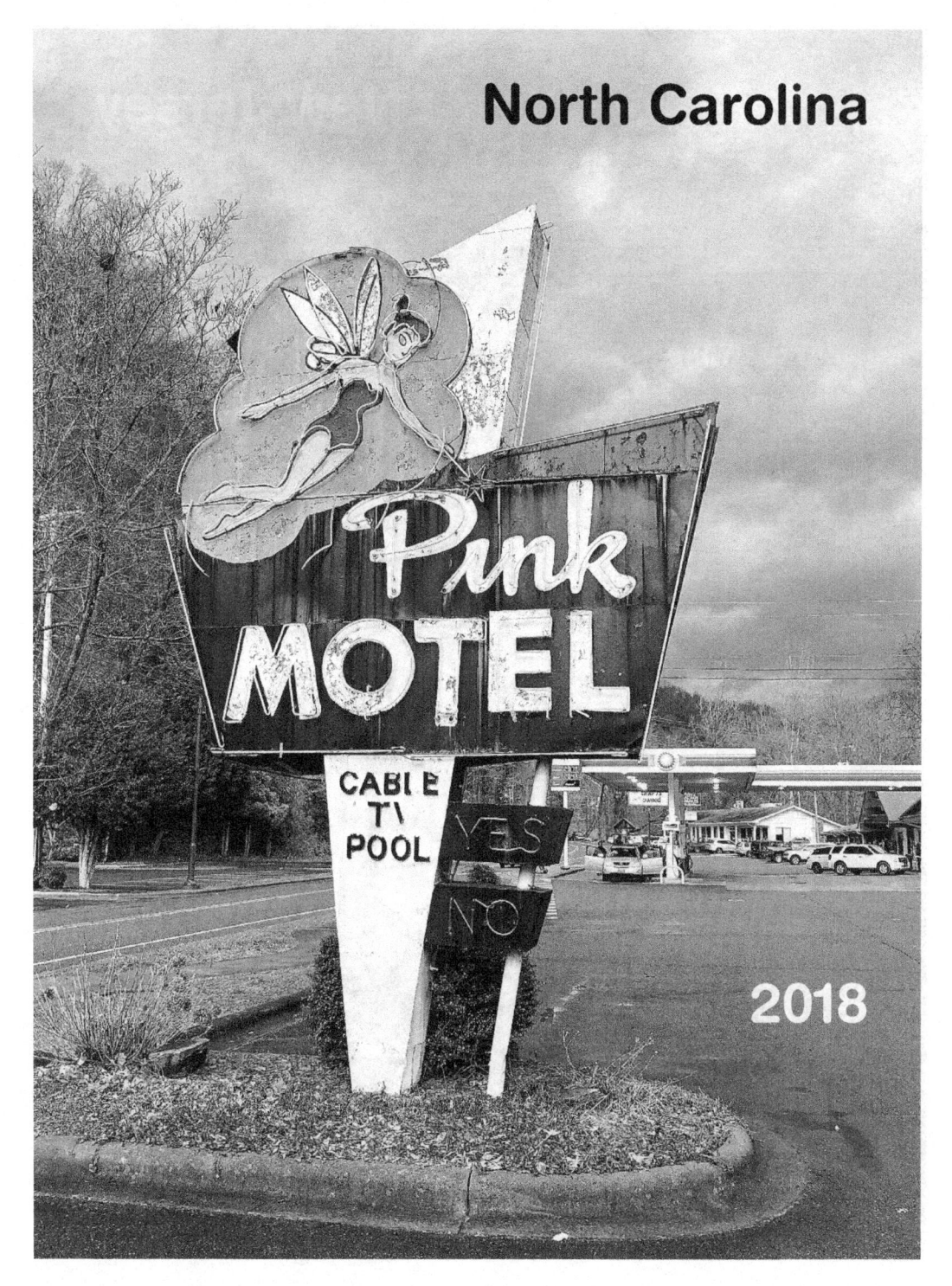

2018

Tinkerbell lit up on U.S. Highway 441 after the Pink Motel opened in 1953

Warren LeMay

STEPHEN H. PROVOST

New Jersey

early 1900s

A glowing Gillette razor and a Woolworth sign help illuminate the Atlantic City boardwalk

Detroit Publishing Company, Library of Congress

SIGNPOST UP AHEAD, THE EAST

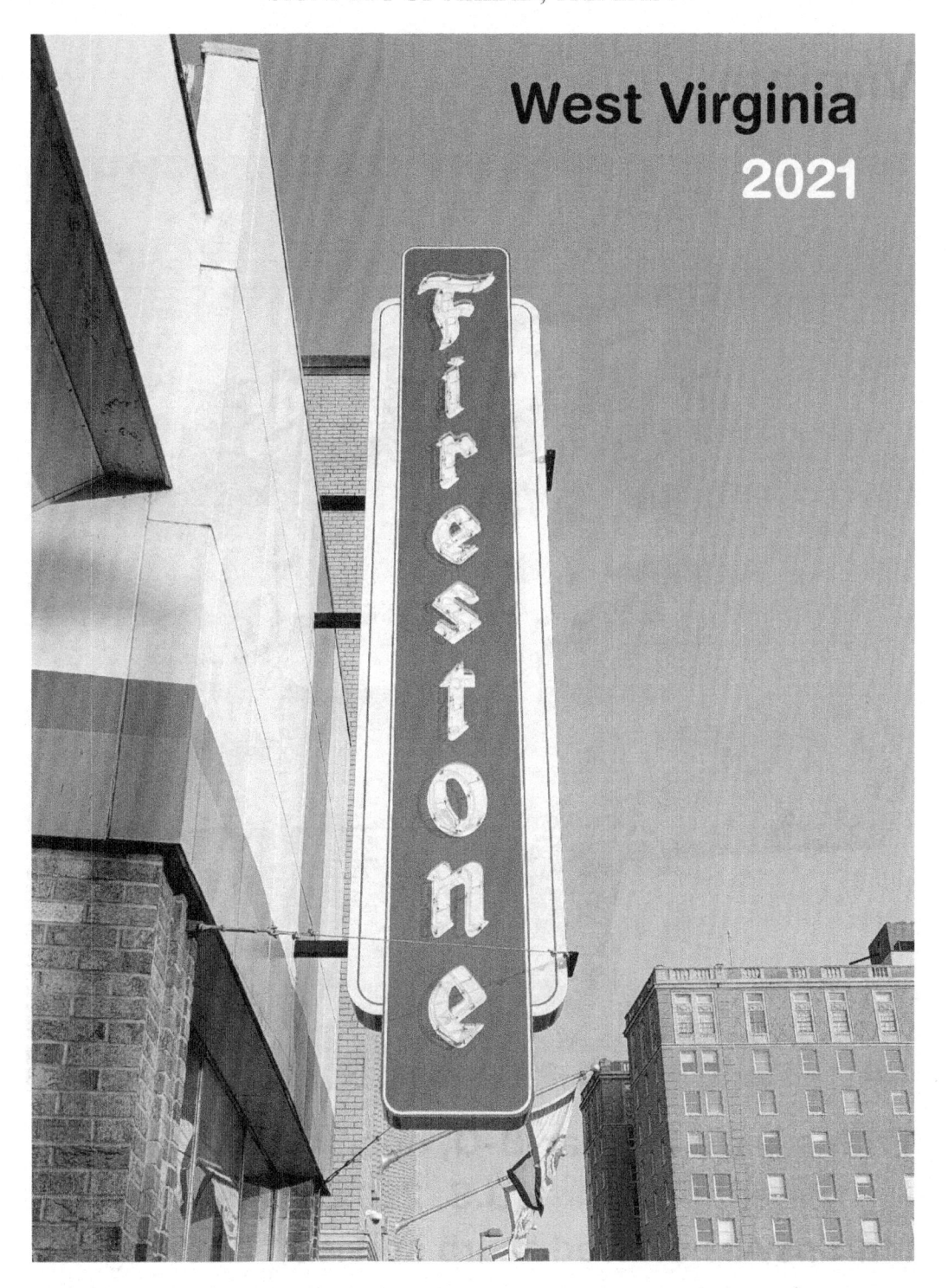

West Virginia
2021

The Firestone Garage on Washington Street in Charleston was the second in the chain

Stephen H. Provost

Virginia 2018

Frith's Dixie Pig Bar-B-Q, open since 1954 on Memorial Boulevard (U.S. 220 Business) in Martinsville offered "curb service," cooking pork shoulders on a wood-and-propane cooker out back

Stephen H. Provost

SIGNPOST UP AHEAD, THE EAST

Florida 1949

Phoenix Loan Corp. in Jacksonville had plenty of neon to capture night drivers' attention

State Library and Archives of Florida

Kentucky
2021

The Twig and Leaf diner was established in 1962, south of Louisville on U.S. Highway 31E

Stephen H. Provost

Ronnie's Coffee Shop, Restaurant, and Bake Shop opened in 1956 on Colonial Drive at Primrose Avenue in Orlando and closed in 1995, serving more than 21 million customers meals like veal cutlet, stuffed cabbage, and matzah balls

State Library and Archives of Florida

North Carolina
1962

Leggett's Department Store used a corner neon sign to attract shoppers in Roanoke Rapids; the Leggett's chain later merged with rival Belk

University of North Carolina Libraries Commons

Henry's Drive-In on Route 66 in Cicero has served hot dogs topped with fries (as depicted on its neon sign) since the 1950s

Stephen H. Provost

North Carolina 1947

Johnny's Drive-In Grill, seen in all its nighttime glory, opened in 1948 and operated on U.S. Highway 1 in Raleigh alongside a motel and supper club; the supper club was destroyed by fire in 1965

Albert Barden, State Archives of North Carolina

Virginia 2018

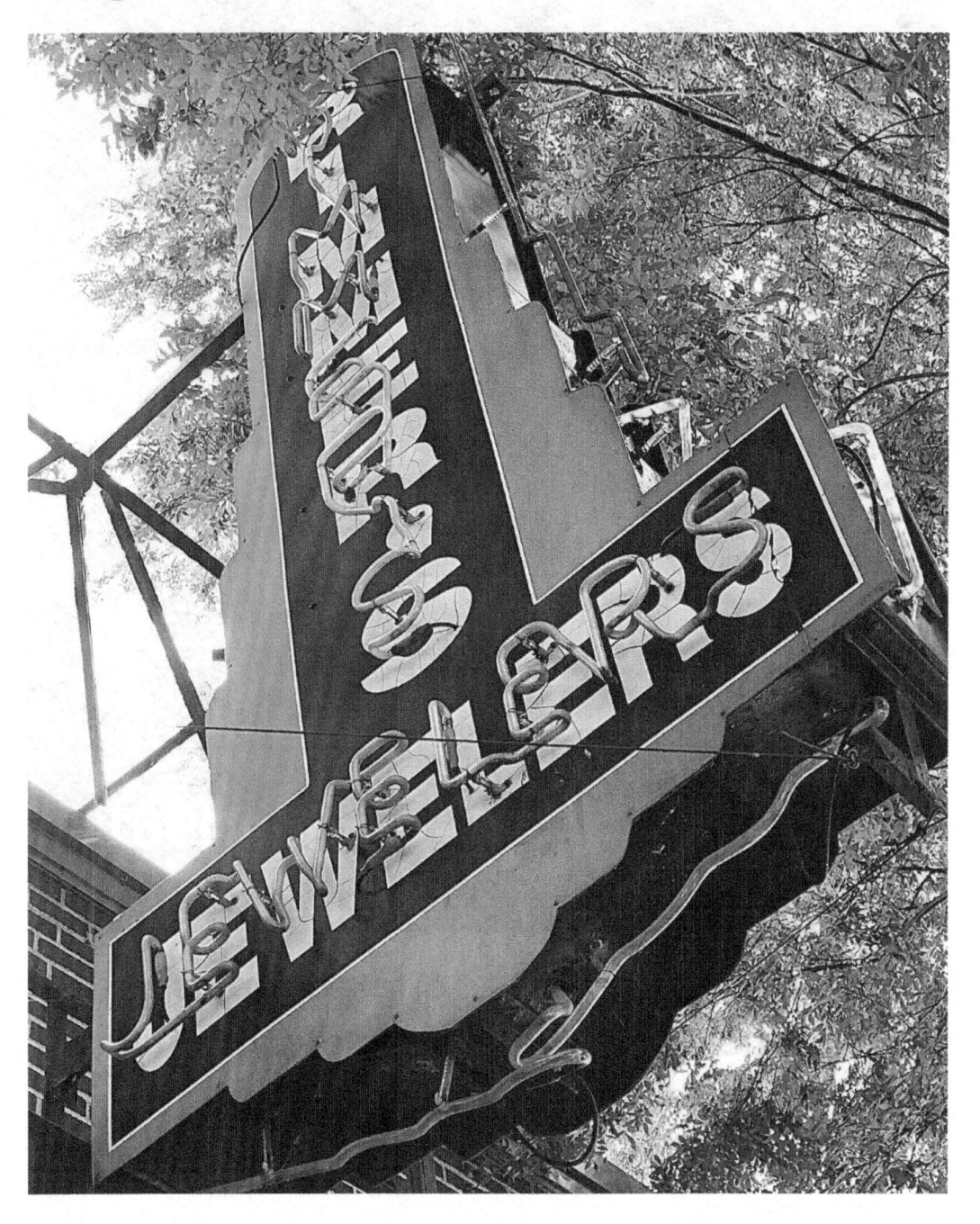

Rimer's Jewelers is long closed, but the neon remains on Main Street in Martinsville

Stephen H. Provost

STEPHEN H. PROVOST

Florida 1961

The Top Hat in Key West offered rooms by the night or the week when this photo was taken in April of 1961

State Library and Archives of Florida

Virginia 2021

This sign on U.S. Highway 11 is all that's left of the Robert E. Lee Motel, which was built in the 1940s between Abingdon and Bristol and was one of the first three places in the country where you could buy Kentucky Fried Chicken

Stephen H. Provost

STEPHEN H. PROVOST

VII

New Heights: Towers of Power

Pennsylvania
1937

A&P's corner stores, such as this one on Federal Street in Pittsburgh, once dominated the U.S. grocery market, but a little extra publicity for products such as Pillsbury flour on a giant rooftop sign never hurt

University of Pittsburgh

SIGNPOST UP AHEAD, THE EAST

Massachusetts 1978

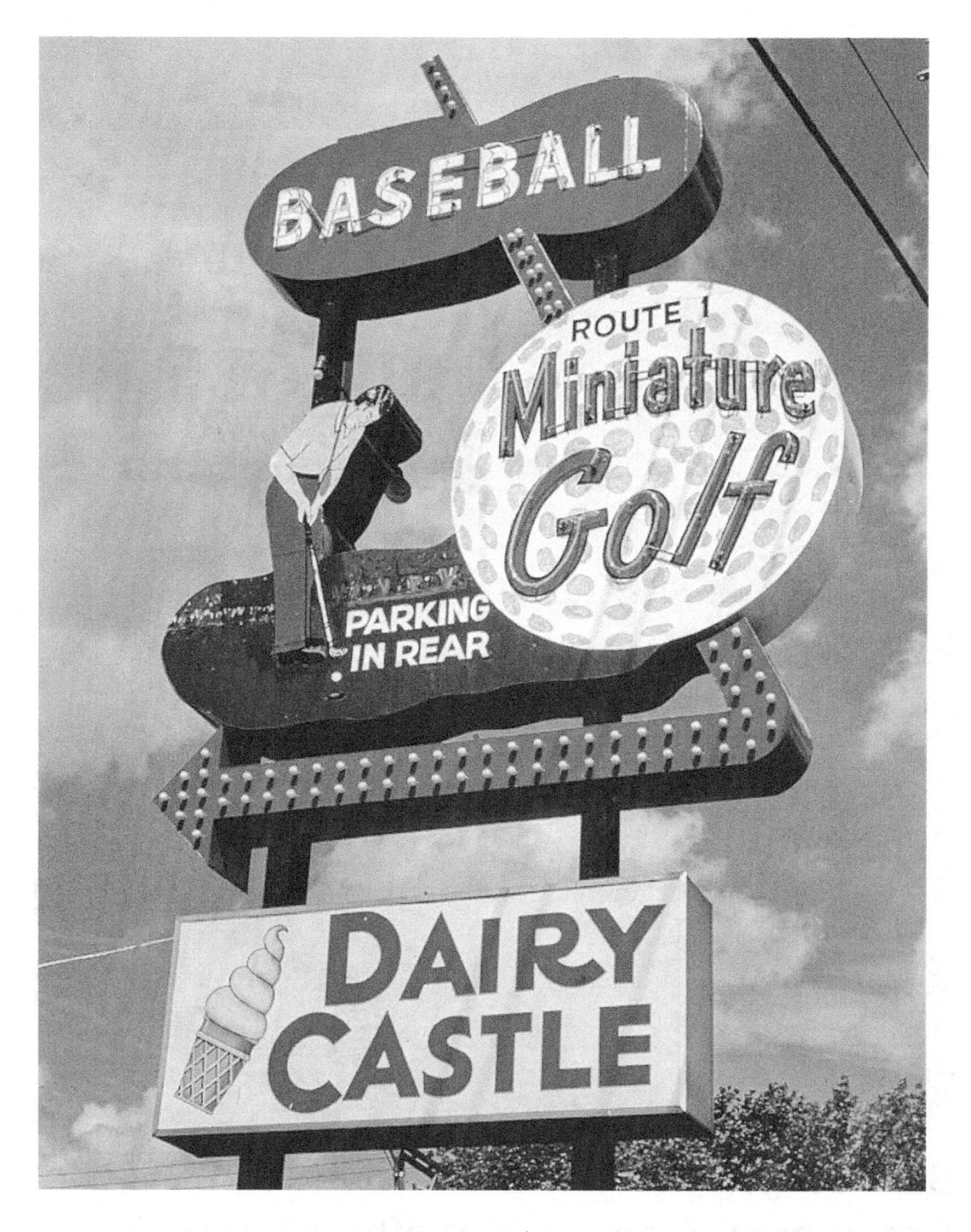

Miniature golf course and ice cream shop on U.S. Highway 1 in Saugus

John Margolies, Library of Congress

STEPHEN H. PROVOST

North Carolina 2022

Beef Burger on Gate City Boulevard in Greensboro closed in 2021 after 57 years in business

Stephen H. Provost

SIGNPOST UP AHEAD, THE EAST

Virginia
1961

Lukhard's Market caught shoppers' eyes with this interestingly shaped sign at the Westbury Shopping Center **in Richmond**

Adolph B. Rice Studio, Library of Virginia

Georgia
2020

Chicken Little, meet Chicken... BIG at this Kentucky Fried Chicken restaurant in Marietta on U.S. Highway 41

Stephen H. Provost

Kentucky 2020

The first KFC, on U.S. Highway 25W in Corbin, started as a gas station in 1930; the present restaurant opened along with a motel in 1939

Stephen H. Provost

STEPHEN H. PROVOST

Maine 1984

Charlie's Diner customers must have gotten a kick out of this sign in Leeds

John Margolies, Library of Congress

Pennsylvania
1913

Even morticians got into the billboard act, with Eaton Co. Undertakers erecting this sign atop a five-story building on Grant and Sixth streets in Pittsburgh

University of Pittsburgh

Virginia 2020

This sign greets shoppers at Roanoke's Towers Shopping Center on Colonial Avenue

Stephen H. Provost

SIGNPOST UP AHEAD, THE EAST

New York 1938

A New York church sent motorists' eyes heavenward with this high-altitude billboard

Dick Sheldon

STEPHEN H. PROVOST

Florida
1926

Coral Gables **Pharmacy, with its big scaffold sign, sold drugs, soda, candy and cigars**

State Library and Archives of Florida

Virginia
2021

An arrow on U.S. Highway 29 in Danville once pointed to something, but it's unclear what

Stephen H. Provost

STEPHEN H. PROVOST

Massachusetts
1984

Planters' Mr. Peanut helped the Half Dollar Bar stand out on U.S. Route 1 in Peabody

John Margolies, Library of Congress

SIGNPOST UP AHEAD, THE EAST

North Carolina 2022

Char-Grill has been serving up burgers, fries, sodas, and shakes on Hillsborough Street in Raleigh since 1959

Stephen H. Provost

STEPHEN H. PROVOST

Illinois
1938

A banner across Main Street in Peoria declares that "what helps business helps you"
Arthur Rothstein, Library of Congress

SIGNPOST UP AHEAD, THE EAST

Ohio 2018

A faded multi-tiered sign on U.S. Highway 52 in Ironton touts "first and last" and "carry out," but the rest is hard to decipher

Stephen H. Provost

Kentucky 2020

Gerry's Roller Rink on the Cumberland Falls Highway, U.S. 25W, has been skating along since the 1950s

Stephen H. Provost

SIGNPOST UP AHEAD, THE EAST

Pennsylvania 1926

This 3-D Marathon Motor Oil sign rose high above Pittsburgh's Forbes Avenue and Boulevard of the Allies

University of Pittsburgh

STEPHEN H. PROVOST

Maine 1984

An udderly ridiculous cow surmounts a sign for the Starlite Restaurant in Old Orchard Beach

John Margolies, Library of Congress

The Eastland Center on U.S. Highway 31E in Kentucky featured this vintage neon tower and clock out front in 2020

Stephen H. Provost

STEPHEN H. PROVOST

Pennsylvania 1984

A Howdy Doody-type character welcomes visitors to Schell's in Reading

John Margolies, Library of Congress

SIGNPOST UP AHEAD, THE EAST

Pennsylvania 1935

An ad for Fort Pitt Beer was in precarious position above Pittsburgh's Bigelow Boulevard

University of Pittsburgh

North Carolina 2021

Visitors could kick off their shoes and "sit a spell" at the Mountaineer Inn on Tunnel Road, serving Asheville since the 1930s

Stephen H. Provost

Virginia 2019

This office supply store on U.S. Highway 11, aka Main Street, in Wytheville has an eye-catching pencil-shaped sign

Stephen H. Provost

West Virginia 2021

A frosty mug of root beer was fitting atop the Huntington Frostop drive-in on State Route 10

Stephen H. Provost

SIGNPOST UP AHEAD, THE EAST

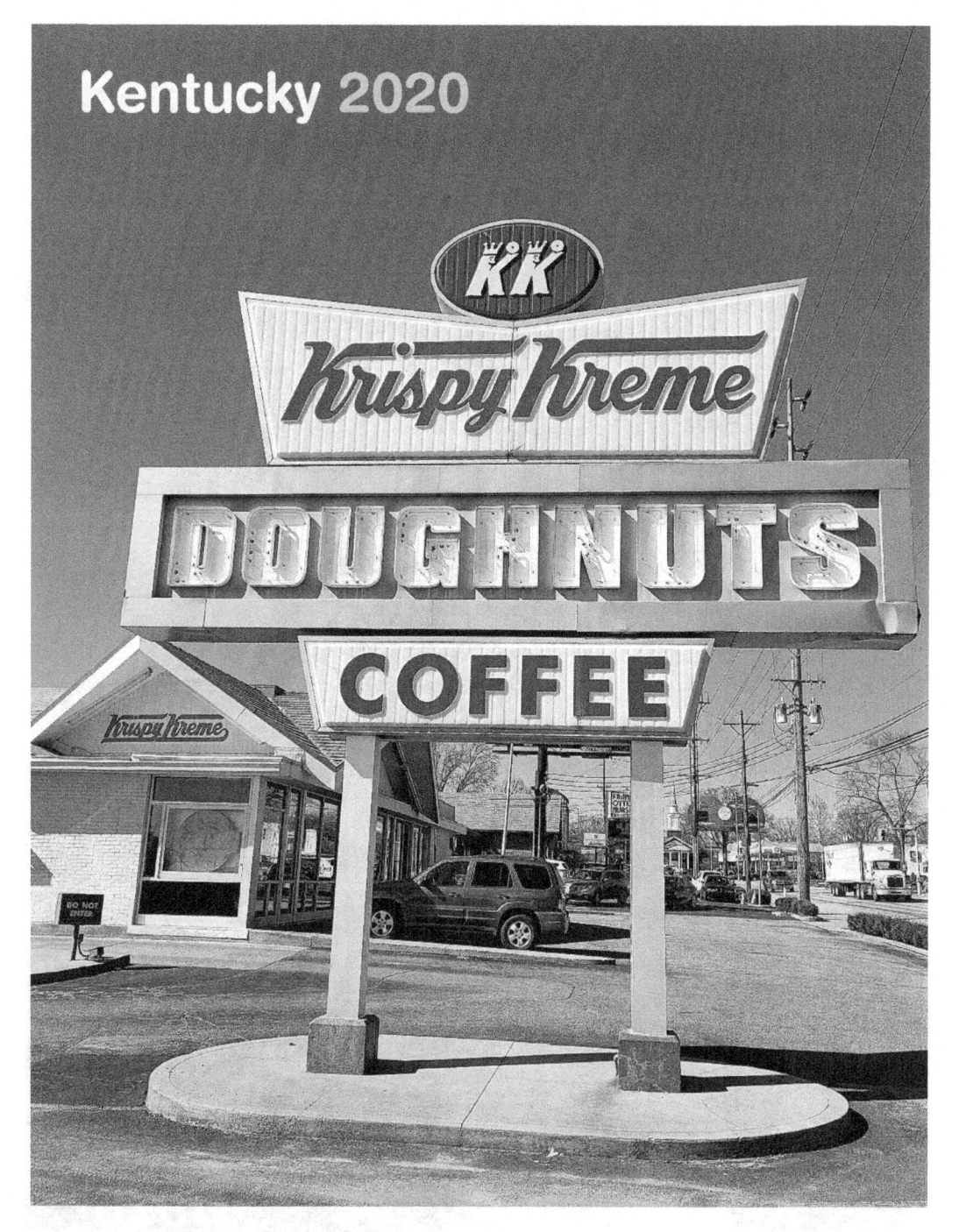

Kentucky 2020

A big pillared sign calls attention to Krispy Kreme Doughnuts on U.S. Highway 31E south of Louisville

Stephen H. Provost

STEPHEN H. PROVOST

Massachusetts

1978

Abbey Motel lighthouse sign, North Attleboro

John Margolies, Library of Congress

South Carolina 2020

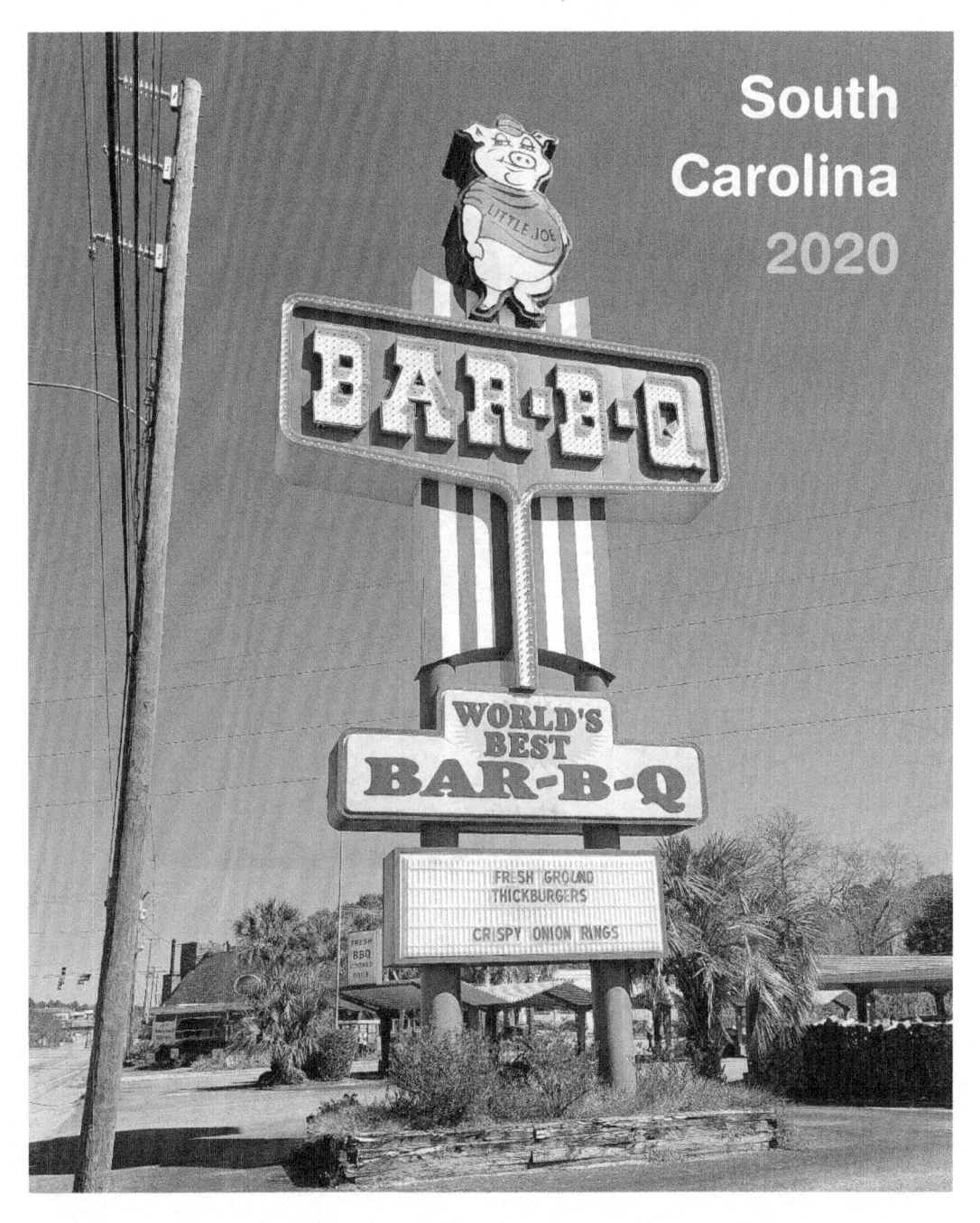

"Little Joe" serves the "world's best bar-b-q," according to this giant lighted sign at Maurice's Piggie Park on the Charleston Highway in West Columbia

Stephen H. Provost

Virginia 2021

Speaking of pigs, Piggly Wiggly, the nation's first self-service market, flagged down drivers on U.S. Highway 58 in Danville with this Porky-esque sign

Stephen H. Provost

SIGNPOST UP AHEAD, THE EAST

Michigan 1942

Sam's Cut Rate was the largest discount store in Detroit — and had one of the largest signs to boot, dwarfing signs for Crawford Clothes and a billboard urging citizens to buy war bonds

Arthur S. Siegel, Library of Congress

Kentucky 2020

Parkette Drive In on Lexington's Circle Road (State Route 4) was closed and torn down in 2022 after more than 70 years serving shrimp, chicken, fish boxes, burgers and more

Stephen H. Provost

South Carolina 2020

Big Irvin stands guard outside Whiteford's Giant Burger, open since 1969 on the U.S. 76 Bypass in Laurens

Stephen H. Provost

North Carolina 2020

The Starlite Motel sign on Andy Griffith Parkway, aka U.S. 52, in Mt. Airy bears a close resemblance to a Holiday Inn sign

Stephen H. Provost

SIGNPOST UP AHEAD, THE EAST

New Jersey
c. 1970

A big tube of toothpaste (what else?) and a giant clock sit atop the Colgate & Company plant in Jersey City

Historic American Engineering Record

North Carolina 2021

Just a few Stuckey's remain from what was once a giant chain; this one can be found paired with a Dairy Queen off I-40 in Old Fort

Stephen H. Provost

SIGNPOST UP AHEAD, THE EAST

Wisconsin

1941

Wisconsin means cheese, as clearly marked by this sign at the Badger Market and Red Crown gas stop on U.S. Route 41 in Kenosha County

John Vachon, Library of Congress

Kentucky 2020

The Holiday Motel in Cave City, not to be confused with the Holiday Inn, sits on U.S. 31E, historically known as the Dixie Highway

Stephen H. Provost

Virginia
2019

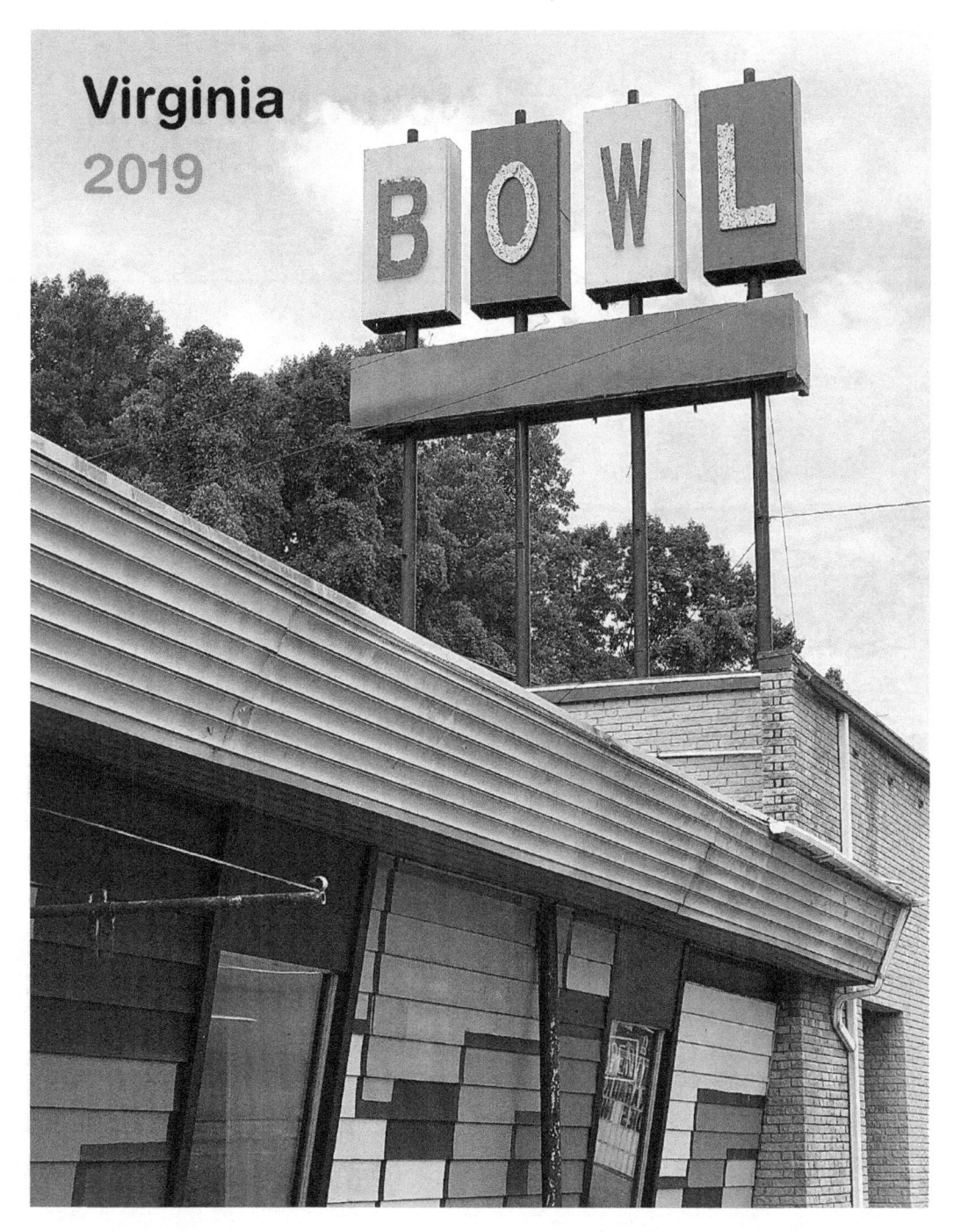

Travelers on Business U.S. 220 who want to stop for some recreation and a burger can do so at Sportlanes in Martinsville

Stephen H. Provost

R.J. Reynolds Tobacco used its smokestacks in Winston-Salem to advertise its product

Stephen H. Provost

Sunken Gardens botanical gardens off U.S. Highway 92 in St. Petersburg opened to the public in 1936 and still has this sign out front

State of Florida Library and Archives

STEPHEN H. PROVOST

Virginia 2020

Despite its impressive sign, this Shoney's off U.S. Highway 11 and I-81 in Troutville is permanently closed

Stephen H. Provost

SIGNPOST UP AHEAD, THE EAST

Kentucky 2020

Burgers Shakes on Circle Road in Lexington opened its doors around 1957 and was still charging just $1.23 for a burger in 2020

Stephen H. Provost

No, it's not Vegas, baby. But this Horseshoe off U.S. 41 in Hammond, was originally owned by Las Vegas casino operator Jack Binion

Stephen H. Provost

SIGNPOST UP AHEAD, THE EAST

Virginia 2020

This iconic Dr Pepper sign went up in the 1940s in downtown Roanoke

Stephen H. Provost

STEPHEN H. PROVOST

South Carolina 2020

You'll actually find this giant sign at a huge roadside attraction south of the North Carolina state line at U.S. 501 and 301, and I-95

Stephen H. Provost

About the author

Stephen H. Provost has written several books about life in 20th century America, including numerous books on America's highways. During more than three decades in journalism, he has worked as a managing editor, copy desk chief, columnist and reporter at five newspapers. Now a full-time author, he has written on such diverse topics as dragons, mutant superheroes, mythic archetypes, language, department stores and his hometown. Visit him online and read his blogs at stephenhprovost.com.

Did you enjoy this book?

Recommend it to a friend. And please consider rating it and/or leaving a brief review online at Amazon, Barnes & Noble and Goodreads.

Also by the author

Works of Fiction

    The Talismans of Time (Academy of the Lost Labyrinth, Book 1)
    Pathfinder of Destiny (Academy of the Lost Labyrinth, Book 2)
    Memortality (The Memortality Saga, Book 1)
    Paralucidity (The Memortality Saga, Book 2)
    The Only Dragon
    Identity Break
    Feathercap
    Nightmare's Eve

Works of Nonfiction

    Yesterday's Highways
    America's First Highways
    Highway 99: The History of California's Main Street
    Highway 101: The History of El Camino Real
    Happy Motoring!
    Highways of the South
    The Lincoln Highway in California (with Gary Kinst)
    Victory Road
    Mark Twain's Nevada
    The Great American Shopping Experience
    Martinsville Memories
    Fresno Growing Up
    The Century Cities series:

        Cambria Century, Carson City Century, Charleston Century, Danville Century, Fresno Century, Goldfield Century, Greensboro Century, Huntington Century, Roanoke Century, San Luis Obispo Century

STEPHEN H. PROVOST

Praise for other works

"If you have any interest in highways, old diners and motels and such, or 20th century US history, this book is for you. It is without a doubt one of the best highway books ever published."
— Dan R. Young, Highway 101 historian, on **Yesterday's Highways**

"Both books are well-researched, nicely written, and illustrated with good black and white photographs, and both contribute importantly to highway literature."
— Wayne Shannon, *Jefferson Highway Declaration*,
on **Yesterday's Highways** and **America's First Highways**

"... an engaging narrative that pulls the reader into the story and onto the road. ... I highly recommend **Highway 99: The History of California's Main Street**, whether you're a roadside archaeology nut or just someone who enjoys a ripping story peppered with vintage photographs."
— Barbara Gossett,
Society for Commercial Archaeology Journal

"Profusely illustrated throughout, **Highway 99** is unreservedly recommended as an essential and core addition to every community and academic library's California History collections."
— California Bookwatch

"... it contains a lot of information I hadn't heard before. Both books prove well-written with few weaknesses..."
— Ron Warnick, route66news.com,
on **Yesterday's Highways** and **America's First Highways**

"An essential primer for anyone seeking an entrée into the genre. Provost serves up a smorgasbord of highlights gleaned from his personal memories of and research into the various nooks and crannies of what 'used-to-be' in professional team sports."
— Tim Hanlon, Good Seats Still Available,
on **A Whole Different League**

STEPHEN H. PROVOST

"As informed and informative as it is entertaining and absorbing, **Fresno Growing Up** is very highly recommended for personal, community, and academic library 20th Century American History collections."
— John Burroughs, Reviewer's Bookwatch

"The complex idea of mixing morality and mortality is a fresh twist on the human condition. ... **Memortality** is one of those books that will incite more questions than it answers. And for fandom, that's a good thing."
— Ricky L. Brown, Amazing Stories

"Punchy and fast paced, **Memortality** reads like a graphic novel. ... (Provost's) style makes the trippy landscapes and mind-bending plot points more believable and adds a thrilling edge to this vivid crossover fantasy."
— Foreword Reviews

"The genres in this volume span horror, fantasy, and science-fiction, and each is handled deftly. ... **Nightmare's Eve** should be on your reading list. The stories are at the intersection of nightmare and lucid dreaming, up ahead a signpost ... next stop, your reading pile. Keep the nightlight on."
— R.B. Payne, Cemetery Dance

"**Memortality** by Stephen Provost is a highly original, thrilling novel unlike anything else out there."
— David McAfee, bestselling author of
33 A.D., 61 A.D., and *79 A.D.*

"Provost sticks mostly to the classics: vampires, ghosts, aliens, and even dragons. But trekking familiar terrain allows the author to subvert readers' expectations. ... Provost's poetry skillfully displays the same somber themes as the stories. ... Worthy tales that prove external forces are no more terrifying than what's inside people's heads."
— Kirkus Reviews on **Nightmare's Eve**

"The story feels so close, so intimate, we as readers experience the emotions, the events, and the conflicts, in what feels like real time. Gut-wrenchingly so."
— Stephen Mark Rainey, author of *Blue Devil Island*, on **Death's Doorstep**

Made in the USA
Monee, IL
10 June 2025